Praise for No Big Deal

I've known Dean Brownrout, the art dealer, for over 15 years. Until now, he's been so tight-lipped about his experiences in the music business you'd think he was in witness protection. I had no idea. None. *No Big Deal* is a fascinating, laugh-out-loud funny, nostalgic, and sometimes tragic account of unbridled ambition (not only his!) and an industry in flux.

> —**Janz Castelo de Armas**, founder and artistic director
> Buffalo Chamber Players and Buffalo Philharmonic
> Orchestra violist

A great read! I found the book interesting—and full of Dean's sly wit. While Dean and I traveled separate paths until meeting in the '90s, I can relate to a lot of it. *No Big Deal* touches on familiar themes; the New York stuff is particularly evocative. The book made me smile, and also brought back the rollercoaster of emotions from the end of my own music business career. It's both an honest, unvarnished portrayal of the independent record business at the end of the 20th century, and a well-told personal tale that manages to steer away from showbiz clichés and tropes.

> —**John Lay**, former co-manager Squeeze, Jools Holland,
> former manager, Robyn Hitchcock & The Egyptians,
> The Greenberry Woods

As a rock musician, I was always an outsider, pressing my nose against the plate glass window of the music biz, which was totally bewildering to me and other hopefuls. Now we finally get to see what the hell was up on the *other* side. With *No Big Deal*, you get a front row seat in the sexy late 20th century music industry boom, which you'll witness falling apart slowly, poignantly, as the digital age rears its pointy microhead to destroy the gleaming towers of Oz. The book is a thoroughly enjoyable, great read, impossible to put down. It's quite witty, and funny, too. Zipping through the book, you'll be too busy gulping down the juicy anecdotes to stop and take stock of the author's natural storytelling gifts. For entertainment industry newbies, it's golden manna: a master class in wheeling and dealing, and how to fully enjoy the fruits of *others'* labors. More importantly, it also demonstrates how to bounce back from setbacks, using them as a joyous springboard to bigger things. Infuriatingly, the author was at the right place at the right time, like, *a million times*. He peels off more band names than the Rock & Roll Hall of Fame roster, and got to casually rub shoulders with the likes of Jagger, Richards, Dylan, Grace Jones, and Michael Jackson. Now *that's* a memoir. He should start his own trading card collection. And I'll definitely be sending him my medical bill for injuries sustained from chronic jaw-dropping.

—**Alan Lord**, author of *High Friends in Low Places*

An entertainingly fond memoir, Dean's story doubles as a cautionary tale about the "business" side of the music business. It made me nostalgic for the pre-internet record industry: CDs, brick-and-mortar record stores, and BMX Bandits' first US tour.

—**Francis Macdonald**, drummer, BMX Bandits,
Teenage Fanclub

In Dean Brownrout's story of progress from the rock & roll wilderness of Buffalo, NY to ground zero of New York City's scuzzy clubs and snazzy boardrooms … *No Big Deal* is wild, woolly, crazy, and clearly driven by the fun of it all. … There are eight million stories in the naked city of rock & roll, and this is one worth knowing.

—**Ira Robbins**, cofounder, *Trouser Press* magazine

I found *No Big Deal* addicting. As Dean documents his rise through the music business, he provides a rare look behind the curtain. What's revealed is not always pretty; you're there for the ups and downs, the triumphs and heartbreaks. The story is strewn with colorful characters—it's a fascinating and insightful ride from the indie '80s to the bloated '90s, and the eventual crumbling of the record business, as the digital age creeps in.

—**Michael Shelley**, WFMU DJ and former Big Deal
recording artist

Who remembers, who forgets, who writes it down, and in which way? Reading Dean's memoir offers a glimpse, a reflection, a brain's eye view, a perspective, a well-written and engaging story in the line leading to where we find ourselves now. It's a pandemic-fueled inner vision of someone who was there back then, who contributed and was in the mix of the NY and global music scene, who had taste and know-how. It's a Big Deal, for sure.

—**Robert Singerman**, former manager, The Fleshtones,
The Smithereens, Gipsy Kings, former agent, R.E.M.,
Violent Femmes

NO BIG DEAL

*Chasing the indie music dream
in the last days of the record business*

GUERNICA WORLD EDITIONS 81

NO BIG DEAL

*Chasing the indie music dream
in the last days of the record business*

DEAN BROWNROUT

Foreword by Ira Robbins of Trouser Press

GUERNICA
World
EDITIONS

TORONTO–CHICAGO–BUFFALO–LANCASTER (U.K.)
2024

Guernica Editions Founder: Antonio D'Alfonso

Michael Mirolla, editor
Cover design: Allen Jomoc, Jr.
Interior design: Jill Ronsley, suneditwrite.com

Guernica Editions Inc.
1241 Marble Rock Rd., Gananoque (ON), Canada K7G 2V4
2250 Military Road, Tonawanda, N.Y. 14150-6000 U.S.A.
www.guernicaeditions.com

Distributors:
Independent Publishers Group (IPG)
600 North Pulaski Road, Chicago IL 60624
University of Toronto Press Distribution (UTP)
5201 Dufferin Street, Toronto (ON), Canada M3H 5T8

First edition.
Printed in Canada.

Legal Deposit—Third Quarter
Library of Congress Catalog Card Number: 2023952727
Library and Archives Canada Cataloguing in Publication
Title: No big deal : chasing the indie music dream in the last days of the
record business / Dean Brownrout ; foreword by Ira Robbins of Trouser Press.
Names: Brownrout, Dean, author | Robbins, Ira A., author of introduction etc.
Series: Guernica world editions (Series) ; 81.
Description: 1st edition. | Series statement: Guernica world editions ; 81
Identifiers: Canadiana (print) 20230621597 | Canadiana (ebook)
20240281268 | ISBN 9781771839099 (softcover) | ISBN 9781771839105 (EPUB)
Subjects: LCSH: Brownrout, Dean | LCSH: Concert agents—United
States—Biography. | LCSH: Sound recording executives and producers—
United States—Biography.
Classification: LCC ML429.B87 A3 2024 | DDC 781.49092—dc23

For Jana

"You don't know who I am, but somehow, indirectly, you've been affected by things I did."

—Tony Conrad

Author Note

THIS WORK depicts actual events in the author's life as recollected. The author has recreated experiences and conversations from memories of them. The author has likely retold some conversations in a way that makes him look better and smarter than he is, yet still evokes the feeling and meaning of what was said. Some episodes have been compressed. This book may contain cultural and social elements which by today's informed standards would be considered offensive. While the author has made every effort to ensure that the facts and information in this book were correct at press time, the author does not assume—and hereby disclaims—any liability to any party for any loss, damage, or disruption caused by errors and omissions.

Foreword

INDIE LABELS, those shoestring fiefs of plucky idiosyncrasy that popped up across America in the 1970s, had been lighting up the rock scene for nearly two decades when Dean Brownrout's Big Deal hung out its shingle in New York City in 1993. The fulfillment of a career dream by a veteran heavy metal booking agent and label manager—but devoted to an entirely different type of music—Big Deal released records by Japanese punk-poppers Shonen Knife, future Brian Wilson sidemen the Wondermints, tuneful Chicago rockers Enuff Z'Nuff, Haircut 100 mastermind Nick Heyward, California's eternally adolescent Rubinoos and other pop-oriented outfits largely unknown to the *Billboard Hot 100*.

Those twenty years had brought revolutionary changes to the music world, the most impactful being MTV, which had assumed the make-or-break role of a national Top 40 radio station. Thanks to exposure on the cable channel, promotional videos had supplanted the commercial supremacy of the perfect single. And, thanks in large part to exposure on MTV, Nirvana's 1991 breakthrough had elevated previously small-time labels like Sub Pop into credible advance scouts for the Next Big Thing.

Through it all, indie pop bands carried on in their own small way, unencumbered by debilitating concerns about mega-sales, arena shows, *Video Music Awards* or *Rolling Stone* covers. Although the mainstream occasionally opened its golden gates to the sound (Dwight Twilley, the Romantics, Bangles, Go-Go's, Lemonheads), it has never been a reliable pathway to commercial success. The popularity implicit in power pop's name remained as much ironic as hoped-for.

Of all the label's releases (nearly a hundred between 1993 and 1999), the records that made Big Deal a big deal for me and other fans of Rickenbacker guitars, catchy melodies, chewy choruses, handclaps, and romantic yearning were the four volumes of *Yellow Pills* compiled by St. Louis fanzine publisher Jordan Oakes. For power pop, a narrow genre whose blurry boundaries have sparked countless critical debates (Did the Who invent it? Are the Raspberries and the Knack too concupiscent to be eligible? Or are they the archetype of the form? Does Cheap Trick qualify? Tom Petty? Is pop-punk a bar chord too far?), at least five books attempting to explain it (a recent example being 2021's *Go Further: More Literary Appreciations of Power Pop*), and a documentary film that's been in the works for around a decade, *Yellow Pills* is the genre's *Nuggets*, a document for the ages that shows, not tells, what power pop is all about.

Actually, a lot of what power pop is about is nostalgia, and therein lies the problem. Whether it's the Beatles' enduring and overpowering influence, the Byrds' folkier factor or the sideways spin of Big Star, the form tends to attract revivalists who don't add much to recreating a strain of music they grew up on. Others, however, keep their inspirations better hidden and advance the form with ideas of their own. (In 1995 Britain, a version of that conceptual split was writ large in the Oasis/Blur battle royale, but I'm thinking here more about bands like Shoes, Velvet Crush, Heavenly, the Nerves, Jags, Primitives, Plimsouls, Fountains of Wayne …)

Like so many other small companies founded by enthusiastic idealists, Big Deal didn't last, but the music it midwifed is still out there. And like so many other enthusiastic idealists who put themselves in the picture, Big Deal founder Dean Brownrout worked his way through the music business maze with audacity, ingenuity, hard work, late nights, spilled drinks, and random opportunities. In his story of progress from the rock & roll wilderness of Buffalo, New York to ground zero of New York City's scuzzy clubs and snazzy boardrooms, some of it is painful to imagine, some of it difficult to believe, but *No Big Deal* is wild, woolly, crazy, and clearly driven by the fun of it all.

The perceived glamor and excitement of rock & roll can be a powerful aphrodisiac to those in its thrall. Many become musicians to create it, some become writers to reflect it, still others put themselves in offices, providing the business acumen and stamina to do the impossible: find, promote, present, and manage musicians. There are eight million stories in the naked city of rock & roll, and this is one worth knowing.

Ira Robbins

Prologue:
September 1983, Buffalo, New York

It was definitely time to go. Not just leave the bar—but leave this town.

I'm at the Continental—the local two-floor "new wave" club in downtown Buffalo. The owner, "Bud" Burke, is chasing his boyfriend down the stairs, throwing punches at him, some connecting. Bud's toupee is half-askew. He's been drinking Miller beer all night. I barely notice. It's another typical closing hour at the bar. I'm 21, making $75 to $100 a week plus all the booze I can drink, promoting concerts at this place.

I've been booking local and national acts in the area for the past few years. These were the glory days of new wave and punk rock in America. And Buffalo, like many cities around the country, had a vital live music scene.

My first show at the Continental featuring a nationally recognized artist was in April of the previous year, with the Los Angeles punk band Fear. I'd heard they would be playing an hour away, in Rochester, NY. I called their agent and easily talked him into adding another date to their itinerary.

A bartender at the club dabbled in local music promotion under the name Closet Punk Productions. With $500 to pay the act, we partnered on presenting the event, which we aggressively billed as "Fear: The band that destroyed *Saturday Night Live*."

It's true Fear was banned from *SNL* after a 1981 Halloween appearance. The band was booked at the request of fan John

Belushi. During their performance, they used obscene language and the "friends" they'd brought with them wrecked the set in a slam-dancing frenzy. The situation was so out of control that *SNL* cut to a commercial, while they were playing, to avoid further damage.

On the day of the sold-out show in Buffalo, we found ourselves anticipating the group's arrival; they were now more than an hour overdue for their 3 p.m. soundcheck.

I called their agent.

"We're waiting for Fear," I said. "Do you know when they'll be here?"

"Oh, I'm sure they're on their way."

I wasn't reassured. He asked me to hold. Minutes passed. He returned to the line. "Ummm … they just left New York City."

With no traffic (and no cops), New York to Buffalo is a minimum six-hour drive. Any number of factors, like leaving at rush hour, going the speed limit, or stopping for gas could easily extend the journey to eight hours. It was 4:30. They likely wouldn't arrive until midnight.

We put the opening act on late and drew out their set. The crowd was agitated. Word was spreading that Fear hadn't even arrived. Their van pulled up as people started demanding refunds.

Instruments in hand, the rattled musicians cut through the audience, jumped on stage, and plugged in. I followed them, grabbing the microphone, to shouts of "It's about time!" and "You lucky bastard!"

Overcome with relief, I shouted: "Please welcome the band that destroyed *Saturday Night Live* … FEAR!" And leapt off the stage directly into the oncoming surge of stud-and-dog-collar-wearing audience members. They rewarded me with a flurry of kicks and punches to the midsection.

Setting the stage

My love of popular culture developed as a child of the 1960s and '70s, in a suburb outside of Buffalo, NY.

On TV, I watched *Lost in Space*, *Get Smart*, *The Green Hornet* with Bruce Lee as Kato, *The Mod Squad*, *It Takes a Thief*, *Land of the Giants*, and *The Monkees*. My *Man From U.N.C.L.E.* attaché case was filled with codebreaking wonders and weapons of destruction, allowing me to conduct secret operations around the house. I'm sure my mother, a stay-at-home hysteric, appreciated my stealth attacks and random cap gun sprays at invisible enemies.

At age 5 and 6, the Beatles' *Sgt. Pepper's Lonely Hearts Club Band* album and their animated film *Yellow Submarine* intrigued me. I remember hearing about their breakup when I was 8. Aww, heck, I was just getting to know you guys.

And my entrepreneurial bent was formed at the feet of my father. In 1959, at age 22, he had the foresight to open the first McDonald's franchise in New York State—only *the ninety-third in the world*. The bank was reluctant to lend him the money he needed because they couldn't "find enough information on this 'McDonald's' company."

On Saturdays, he would take me on his rounds, then to lunch and a movie.

I got my earliest taste of clubs and showbiz on those Saturday outings. Dad liked to drop in and chat with neighboring business owners along Niagara Falls Boulevard, where his McDonald's was located. Back then, the thoroughfare connecting Buffalo with nearby Niagara Falls wasn't the commercial sprawl that it is to-day; the McDonald's sat on a patch of asphalt, surrounded by acres of undeveloped land. Dad and I visited restaurants and nightclubs dotted among the no-tell motels and tourist information huts. I'd belly up to the bar and be offered a kiddie cocktail or ask for a Vernors soda—"pop" in local parlance. Lounge bands and singers practiced while I fished out maraschino cherries from the condiment holders when no one was looking.

For the movies we attended, parental ratings were mere suggestions. No subject was off limits. The films of the period often involved an armed biker gang riding through neatly carved paths in the jungles of Vietnam to win the war, or a Vietnam vet exacting vigilante justice for some perceived or actual slight. More sensitive and realistic portrayals of the Vietnam conflict were still a few years out.

I saw all the early James Bond movies in rerelease in the theater, and, at age 7, *On Her Majesty's Secret Service* in first-run. We went to *2001: A Space Odyssey*, *Bullitt*, *Where Eagles Dare*, and *Butch Cassidy and the Sundance Kid*. One of the first singles I ever bought was its theme song, "Raindrops Keep Fallin' on My Head." I played it repeatedly at home until my parents could take it no more.

Still, I frequently asserted my age-appropriate needs. We also saw Disney flicks like *The Love Bug*, *The Barefoot Executive*, and *The Computer Wore Tennis Shoes*.

And where was my mother through all of this? She's a bit of a mythomaniac. In her mind, she was a gourmet cook, telling stories of glorious feasts she spent all day preparing. They all ended with her emerging triumphant and elegant with a perfect platter of roasted meat. I honestly don't remember her cooking a single meal, unless you count watery oatmeal, Kraft Mac & Cheese, and Old El Paso taco kits, which I don't. I mean, she must have fed me. I survived. We ate out a lot. My father being in the food industry helped. He brought home sacks of McDonald's hamburgers, Filet-O-Fish, and bulk foodstuffs.

Mayhem followed Mom; nothing was simple or without drama. Even the most minor activity could have a major impact.

One hot summer day, when I was 7 years old, she had a hankering for ice cream. Her car must have been in the shop, or Dad wasn't around, because she made the extremely poor decision to "borrow" his new two-ton, tri-black, limited-production 1969 Dodge Charger 500 with a tire-smoking 426 HEMI engine nestled under its long, sculpted hood. That's right, for a quick trip to Dairy Queen. What did I know? I was getting ice cream. I hopped into the back seat, and my grandmother eased into the front passenger side.

Mom drove the short distance. The Dairy Queen was a classic drive-up shack on a major thoroughfare. A spot was available right in front. The usual assortment of families, couples, and sugar fiends lined up. Through the nearly floor-to-ceiling plate glass windows, I could see an efficient hive of teen employees bustling about while the owner worked the cash register, relaying cups and cones to customers. Mom took our orders, then popped out of the car. For some reason, she left the engine running.

What happened next is legend, at least in my mind. Maybe she thought she'd already put the car in park? Her focus on procuring the sweet stuff made her even loopier than usual. Whatever the reason, as Mom got in line, she turned to see the hulking muscle car, containing her son and non-driving mother, slowly rolling further into the parking space, where she had just carelessly left it (and us).

She could have simply and quickly traversed the five yards back to the car and thrown it into park. But instead, my mom yelled, "MOTHER!" My grandmother, who lived in NYC half of her life, had never bothered to get a driver's license. Still, having a basic understanding of how cars work, and panicked by her daughter's shrieking, she managed to heave her left leg over the central hump, where her foot landed *on the accelerator*. The DQ owner, alerted by the commotion, an ice cream in each hand, stared open-mouthed at the moving vehicle. The car jerked forward, hit the parking block, jumped it, and sailed through the window, taking most of the concrete building support and a soft-serve machine with it. It came to a stop halfway in and halfway out of the Dairy Queen, surrounded by broken glass and shocked people. I was still in the back seat, waiting for my cone.

In addition to fast cars, Dad loved British television detective and spy shows. Anybody else remember Roger Moore and Tony Curtis in *The Persuaders!*? (I include the exclamation point purposefully and accurately. It totally connotes excitement.) He took family photos with an aluminum Minox B camera that fit easily into the palm of your hand. It was a favored tool of Cold War espionage operatives. I am still an Anglophile when it comes to TV and film.

Dad's voracious reading habit found him constantly consuming thriller novels. To this day, he always has a paperback in hand, usually by someone with a hyper-masculine *nom de plume* and an equally over-the-top jacket photo—collar-up bomber jacket or safari shirt, anybody? Judging by the books Dad carries around, the late Robert Ludlum is still writing. I inherited his love of reading, though I have long grown weary of the ubiquitous plots in his favorite fiction genre—often featuring either a sunken German submarine and perfectly preserved documents pointing to Nazi gold, or the Russians' long game, where they install a sleeper agent in the highest echelons of US government. Oh, wait. Maybe that one isn't fiction.

In the early '70s, my father and I continued to see movies together: *M.A.S.H.*, *Kelly's Heroes*, *The French Connection*, *Day of the Jackal*, *Billy Jack*, *Walking Tall*, and *Sleeper*. Musically, Badfinger's "Day After Day" and the Raspberries' "Go All the Way" were in constant rotation on the household stereo. *The Young Rebels*, *The Partridge Family*, and *Alias Smith and Jones* held my attention on television.

Of my own accord, I'd begun writing to the entertainment critic for the *Buffalo Courier-Express*, criticizing him for failing to understand the latest movie or record. After all, my eleven years on earth had qualified me to render judgment on this long-working journalist, apprising him of the significance of, for example, *Executive Action*, an arid JFK conspiracy theory mash-up. He published many of my letters, often sparring with me or thanking me in print. He sent me a note, encouraging me to write my own capsule film reviews which he printed with other reader's letters.

I still went to films with Dad, but now—with the freedom offered by my bright yellow Schwinn ten-speed bike—I began seeing movies by myself or with friends. On Saturday mornings we'd first cruise the shopping mall, and then hit the cinema, catching titles like *The Sugarland Express* or *McQ*. The poster for *McQ*, a cop revenger starring John Wayne, gave his gun co-billing. *Earthquake* was excitingly presented with amazing new Sensurround technology—the bass made it feel like the whole theater was rumbling. We waited with bated breath to see future classics like *Jaws*, *Star Wars*, and *Close Encounters of the Third Kind*.

The letter-writing continued on and off for years. I even supplied year-end best and worst top-ten lists, which the paper gamely published. In retrospect, my youthful eruditions were farcical, nay, embarrassing. "*Twilight's Last Gleaming* is the best picture of the year." "*Coma* will be viewed as a classic in years to come!" I'm certain I also praised a few other films from that era, like *Marathon Man*, *Network*, and *All the President's Men*. I still stand by my favorable review of *Car Wash*, though my claim that the audience was "dancing in the aisles" may have stretched journalistic credibility.

Buffalo was great for that kind of thing. You were encouraged to fail in public as you learned and figured out what you might want to be. Many of my friends' parents, seeing my "reviews" in print, went to the movies based on my recommendations. Sorry, Mr. and Mrs. Perelstein.

I embraced late-night music television through popular shows like *The Midnight Special* and *Don Kirshner's Rock Concert*. I devoured the pages of *Creem* magazine and *Rolling Stone*, then a newsprint publication. But unlike many teenagers who dreamed of becoming a rock star, I was drawn to the *business* of music. Stories of on-the-make hustlers like David Geffen, or music industry veterans like Ahmet Ertegun of Atlantic Records, fascinated me. Not many teenagers knew, or cared, who Mo Ostin was. (An eminent music business professional, Ostin was inducted into the Rock & Roll Hall of Fame in 2003.)

My interest in TV and film inspired thoughts of a career as a director, but music soon supplanted that—mostly because it seemed more immediately attainable: "You've got a band? I can be your manager." "You've got a venue? Let me book my band there." I was driven by the entrepreneurial gene and an innate sense of opportunity. By the time I was 15, I was managing friends' bands and producing local concerts at community centers and auditoriums.

Before I was old enough to drive, I hustled Todd Rundgren's phone number from a friend of a friend of his car mechanic. I reached him on the phone, and somehow talked him into appearing in concert at a local venue. The show was scrubbed during negotiations, when his agent found out I had just turned 16.

The sounds of free-form and mainstream FM radio also informed my tastes. By the late '70s, as an older teen, I welcomed the exciting introduction of punk and new wave.

I reached my full adult height of 6' 5" in the tenth grade. Because of my size at that young age, people usually thought I was older. I turned that to my advantage, doing what any right-minded teenager would. I went to bars to see bands. With the drinking age only 18, I easily got in. I almost blew it the first time I ordered a drink at one of the city's most notorious dives. Having very little actual drinking experience, I asked for a "Dubonnet and soda." I'd heard Dad order it occasionally. The peroxide blonde server stared vacantly. I quickly recovered, requesting a beer.

Soon after graduating high school in 1980, I was bringing national and international acts like Fear, Billy Idol, Wall of Voodoo, and the Damned into Buffalo-area clubs.

Leaving Buffalo in 1983 for New York City, at 21, I was determined to continue the music-business career I had begun as an enterprising teenager.

Over the next two decades, I progressed from road manager, agent, and manager—working with punk-pioneers

Richard Hell and Johnny Thunders and then-underground metal bands Metallica, Anthrax, Slayer, and Megadeth among others—to running and starting record labels.

The crux of this story begins in the heyday of music on vinyl and cassettes, and transitions through the introduction of compact discs. It ends in the early days of digital music distribution.

My record label, Mercenary Records, an imprint of Celluloid Records, was notable for my signing of unknown Buffalo group the Goo Goo Dolls to their first recording contract.

When Celluloid closed, and with it, Mercenary, I took over as manager for Noise Records' US operation. The German label was a pioneering voice in new metal with such artists as Helloween, Celtic Frost, Kreator, and Voivod.

I then cofounded Big Deal, an independent record label, in my Greenwich Village living room. The label's focus on power pop garnered early recognition; Big Deal was featured on the cover of *Billboard* magazine, the music industry trade bible.

In the mid-'90s, Big Deal merged with a pioneering internet entertainment startup. Paradigm Music Entertainment included one of the web's first large-scale music sites, SonicNet.

With the merger, Big Deal grew to employ a dozen people. At its peak, it occupied offices on New York's swanky Irving Place. In a $30 million stock swap, the combined business was sold to one of the country's largest cable companies: Tele-Communications Inc.

TCI was subsequently sold to AT&T. Without ever having a hit record, Big Deal became a subsidiary of some of the largest media conglomerates in the United States.

If you haven't heard of me, or my former companies, you're not alone. Through the ups and downs, and others' successes, I've made (and lost) several lifetime's worth of earnings.

When you get erased from enough stories, you stop noticing.

Buffalo: 1982-1983

The 4,500-square-foot Continental was owned by Joseph "Bud" Burke. He'd formerly run it as a gay bar, leaning heavily into the S&M lifestyle, which he personally embraced. The club was located in the then-most notorious drug and prostitution district in Buffalo. Two giant German Shepherds named Hitler and Mussolini stood sentinel. In the early '80s, Bud recognized a growing commercial demand for a contemporary music venue, and changed course. He rebranded, establishing the Continental as "Downtown Buffalo's Only All New Wave Nightclub."

His instinct had been right. It quickly became the place to be. He didn't modify the décor or, at the beginning, replace many staffers. Thus, an assortment of hulking bouncers from the leather subculture kept order. In his office, where bands went to get paid, Burke had a rotating bondage suspension rig. In my naiveté, I thought it was an unusual-looking coat rack. And, in his cramped living quarters behind the second-floor bar, he had a videotape collection befitting his predilections. I saw this inner sanctum only once, when he allowed a more popular touring act to use it as a dressing room. With his encouragement, the band was screening some of his "movies." I never went in there again.

———•———

As a result of the Fear show, our reputation as promoters within the developing new wave community grew. At the Continental we secured dates with many artists including Bush Tetras, the Damned, Howard Devoto (Buzzcocks/Magazine), the Dream Syndicate, GBH, the Gun Club, Nina Hagen, Richard Hell, Nona Hendryx, Billy Idol, Medium Medium, the Members, Rank and File, Violent Femmes, and Wall of Voodoo. Bud always offered the traveling band members a hot turkey dinner with all the fixings—a heaven-sent freebie that helped the Continental stand out from other gigs.

The Continental also became a post-concert hangout for musicians playing the area. R.E.M. and the English Beat stopped by, as did David Johansen, after opening for the Who (on their first "farewell tour") at the 70,000-seat Rich Stadium. Johansen's visit was likely more memorable for me than him, as he alternated, in no particular order, between sips of whiskey, amiable conversation, puffs on his cigar, and puking.

———•———

When Billy Idol, touring in support of his eponymous 1982 solo record, rolled through Buffalo, we were lucky enough to be able to promote the event. One of the hot tracks on Idol's album was "White Wedding." Much of the song's success was attributable to frequent airplay on MTV. The cable television network that began as a twenty-four-hour platform for music videos had launched on August 1, 1981.

We arranged for the club staff to be outfitted in cheap white tuxedo jackets with our brand, Billy's name and likeness, and the words "White Wedding" emblazoned on the back. The poster asserted, "formal attire optional." We even brought in a wedding cake. It was a smash with Idol, and his record label.

———•———

Richard Hell was booked to play the club. A pioneering figure at the birth of American punk rock, he was a founding member of Television, and went on to further success with Richard Hell and the Voidoids. Their song "Blank Generation" is widely considered the anthem for the entire punk movement. Despite his moniker, Hell (born Richard Lester Meyers) was actually a well-read and published poet. His angst was more closely aligned with late-nineteenth century French symbolism and the avant-garde than the nihilism of English punk rockers like the Sex Pistols. (The Sex Pistols arguably appropriated Hell's style and attitude then twisted, mashed, and spit it back in a "filth and fury" all their own.)

Following soundcheck, at his nearby hotel, Hell decided to relax with a swim in the indoor pool. A couple of his bandmates were already lounging in a separate whirlpool located at the end of the pool. When Hell saw his group, he excitedly, and inexplicably, dove headfirst into the tub. He hit the shallow bottom, and came up with a gaping, bleeding wound on his forehead.

Rather than going to the hospital—he definitely needed stitches and was most likely concussed—Hell chose to "walk it off." He tended to the cut in his room; it eventually stopped bleeding.

Hell arrived at the Continental and began his performance. Within a few minutes, his wound reopened. Blood streamed down his face and chest. He continued the show. The audience thought it was part of the act. This was what punk rock was supposed to be about, after all.

———•———

I brought a "prestige artist" to town: former Warhol Factory "it girl" and Velvet Underground chanteuse, the German-born Nico. By the early '80s, Nico's star had faded.

The model, actress, and singer was a long way away from her role in Fellini's 1960 masterpiece *La Dolce Vita*, though she still enjoyed a bit of credibility from emerging musicians influenced by her solo recordings and work with the Velvets. Her name recognition and the "curiosity factor" clung to her.

Since the Continental was unavailable, I found a large former 1970s disco above a pizza parlor. The family who owned it was experimenting with different theme nights to try and fill their bar in the new, post-disco world.

Leading up to the engagement, my publicity efforts garnered considerable local press. The day before the show, the star's agent called.

"Dean, I'm afraid Nico can't do the concert. She's in Los Angeles and doesn't want to leave."

My body went numb, then I rallied. "I've got a sold-out show," I said, lying. I desperately wanted the event to occur. Words came spilling out of me. I have no idea what I actually said, but after a few calls back and forth, the date was back on.

She had agreed to come without her band. It would be more of a cabaret presentation. Her agent informed me that she often performed this way and gave me her itinerary—it included a transfer in Chicago to catch her Buffalo flight.

Perhaps out of instinct, I had the presence of mind to ask George Paaswell, a friend from Buffalo who was at college in Illinois, to go to the airport there and make sure she made the transfer. Pre-9/11, you could still greet arriving passengers at the gate.

George leapt at the chance to both meet her, and help me out. He called me as soon as she was aboard.

"Dean, she's a mess and she's very unhappy about having to do this gig," he said.

"Thanks for the warning."

"Dean ... I think she's strung out."

Uh-oh. I knew this was bad. Despite hearing the phrase in movies and television, my suburban background had not taught me exactly what that meant. I thanked him and headed out to the airport to meet the artiste.

(Paaswell's ability to execute similar tasks served him well. He became a Hollywood film and TV producer.)

At the Buffalo arrival gate, the exhausted-looking performer deplaned. The first words out of her mouth were: "I don't know why this show is so important. Why did someone have to meet me in Chicago? I know how to transfer to a plane."

Ignoring that, I smiled, and welcomed her to Buffalo, silently thanking her agent and George for doing what was obviously required to accomplish this miraculous event.

"I had to check my instrument into baggage and I'm really worried," she said.

"Don't worry. We'll sort it all out."

At the baggage claim, a blanket emerged on the carousel.

"Oh … that's mine," Nico said.

Confused but accommodating, I retrieved it. Upset, she let me know the blanket was effectively her "luggage"—she'd wrapped it around her instrument, a harmonium (an early French organ-like instrument) and checked it through.

Broken harmonium parts started passing by. Her panic ramped up, and I retrieved the debris as quickly as I could while being screamed at by Nico. We made a pile of the pieces, and it appeared the main component of the instrument had been (mostly) spared.

Assuring her that we could arrange to have it fixed, with absolutely no clue as to *how*, I ushered her to my car.

As we made the short drive into the city, she was still confused about why this show in Buffalo mattered so much. I thanked her again for coming. I thought things were going … OK.

Then: "You know about my 'problem,' don't you?" she said.

"No, what's that?"

"I need a fix. Heroin."

Oh. My 20-year-old self instantly gathered what "strung out" meant.

"Don't worry. We'll sort this all out," I said, though I knew even less about acquiring heroin than I knew about harmonium repair.

Somehow, I managed to get all of Nico's needs met that day. Hunched over her instrument, her meandering performance was well-received.

Having made a deal with the club owner to finance the night and pay me after costs, post-show I went to the office to collect my take.

"Well, that was great," the owner said. Beside him was a character out of central casting, someone who could, say, break your leg.

"Thanks!" I replied. I was eager for the "payday" and looking forward to further collaboration with the venue. The owner proceeded to reel off a litany of "expenses." By the time it was over I was handed $36—which I handed back to pay my evening's bar tab.

Experiences like this were beginning to lose their allure.

———•———

Throughout 1982 and 1983, I had befriended several touring artists and New York City booking agents. I also earned a reputation as a person who could get things done in the region. I was occasionally asked to tour-manage groups as they made their way around the Northeast, which involved things like driving, acquiring equipment, and arranging for lodging. With Buffalo's proximity to the Canadian border, I was also called upon to help bands cross into Canada for shows in London, Montreal, Ottawa, and Toronto. As a local, organized, clean-cut, and preppily dressed fellow, I provided the perfect counterbalance to the leather-clad band members with their spiked and dyed hairdos. Years later I discovered that my facility for easing border crossings had another subtext, considering the drug problems so many musicians had.

I soon realized I needed to be in New York City, though I had no idea what I'd do when I got there. Bye-bye, Buffalo.

In September 1983, with $500 in my pocket from selling my record collection, and an invitation to sleep on an acquaintance's floor (one of Richard Hell's guitarists, Naux, with whom I had briefly toured), I moved to the city. Well, Jersey City ... but I could see New York from my window.

New York City: A month later

Alot of the hip music companies in New York had offices in the Cable Building at the busy intersection of Broadway and Houston. The Beaux-Arts structure, designed by Stanford White, was the headquarters of a cable car company in 1892. After it was sold in 1925, manufacturers and garment makers moved in. Time took its toll. In the early 1980s, the place was being converted to offices. The building, at 611 Broadway, held a mythical appeal to me. Seeing its return address on correspondence from agents, managers, and publicists had a certain cachet. Kind of like the Brill Building's place in music history, though decidedly more marginal. The location was often mentioned in influential publications like *New York Rocker*. The people who worked inside, and the industry that was taking place there, offered a gateway to the "real" music business. Armed with names and suite numbers of people within, I decided to make it my first stop after exploring my new city for a bit.

Many of the managers and agents I dropped in to visit unannounced were as excited to see me as they were the mouse droppings on their office floors. When I could book their bands in Buffalo, they were happy to talk to me. When I could do nothing for them, and was asking for *their* help in securing a job, it was suggested that I not stop by again without an appointment.

I was especially unsure about calling on Leona Faber, at Crescent Moon Productions. I knew her as an effective agent. She had sold me a show with the Damned, one of a dozen US dates the British punk legends played earlier that year, and the Buffalo concert had been a massive success.

Prior to cofounding Crescent Moon in 1981, Leona had been the publicity director for a New York City club called Hurrah. The former disco (originally known as Harrah) was one of the first large-scale venues to feature punk, new wave, and industrial artists. In the early '70s, the club had also been a prime target of organized crime elements. It was notorious for the interest it received from both the Federal Bureau of Investigation and the New York Federal Strike Force on Organized Crime. And, it was there that Sid Vicious, out on bail for girlfriend Nancy Spungen's murder, smashed a glass into Todd Smith's face. The incident involving Patti Smith's brother sent Vicious back to Rikers for two months.

Still, I didn't know her as well as some of the other agents and managers in the building. When I screwed up my courage to knock on her door, however, she greeted me with open arms. "What a pleasure to meet you," she said. My first impression of her in person was that of a stereotypical New Yorker. "Come in. Everyone, this is Dean Brownrout—he's a wonderful promoter in Buffalo." She emphasized *wonderful*. "What brings you to New York?"

"I moved here. I'm looking for a job—road management, office work, anything you might know of."

"We've got a band going out in a few weeks, and could use a tour manager," she said matter-of-factly.

"Where and when?" I asked, barely containing my joy.

She informed me that Discharge, a critically acclaimed English hardcore punk group formed in 1977, was touring the States and needed someone to look after them. The band, which was also topping UK independent sales charts, had been helped by popular BBC DJ John Peel playing their music on his radio show. Leona hired me on the spot. A month later I was crisscrossing the country with a vanload of mohawk-sporting punks.

———•———

I developed the habit of checking into a hotel or motel before letting anyone catch a glimpse of the guys. While my traditional leather briefcase was covered with the usual assortment of rock & roll touring stickers on the bottom, the top was pristine. I'd set it on the counter at check-in, pop it open and, in combination with my preppy presentation, give the impression that I was a respectable young business traveler. Only when I had the room keys in hand would I shuttle the band through the lobby, often to murmurs of disapproval or open-mouthed shock from employees and guests alike.

In December 1983, heading to Salt Lake City from Denver for a concert, I selected what looked like the shortest route according to the map, and confidently took over the driving duties.

Unfortunately, in this pre-MapQuest world and being a navigational novice, I failed to recognize the paper map's topographic notes. As we passed one jackknifed and abandoned 18-wheeler after another along the icy and snowbound road, we realized we were crossing a section of the Rocky Mountains ... on the cusp of winter ... in a van ill-equipped for that journey. Rigidly focused on the highway before me, I gripped the steering wheel. One band member, glancing out his side window, said: "Whatever you do, don't drive *any further* to your right."

Sliding down the mountain for the better part of a day and night, mostly sideways, we arrived at a town near the bottom of the crossing. I finally unclenched my sphincter.

We eased into a truck stop diner and were greeted with the usual rumblings at the sight of the group. I called Leona from a payphone to let her know our whereabouts. It didn't look like we'd make it to Salt Lake City for that evening's show. Her husband, an experienced tour manager, answered.

"Yes, Leona has been worried. She heard from the promoter in Salt Lake that you're not there yet," he said.

I explained where we were and how we'd arrived there.

"Hell, Dean! I don't even take that route in the summer!"

After rescheduling the performance to the next day, securing accommodations and passing out for the evening, we returned to the same diner in the morning. A loquacious local girl approached our table.

"Are you in a band?"

"Mötley Crüe," I said. The Los Angeles band was just attracting national notice.

"No, you're not!"

"No, really we are," one of the guys said, without attempting to even mask his British accent.

She invited us back to her trailer, asking if we wanted to smoke a joint. We said we had to get back on the road right away and thanked her. Word spread through the diner that we were Mötley Crüe and the patrons decided not to beat us up—this time.

———————•———————

The tour hit California. We stayed at the never-fabulous Tropicana Motel in West Hollywood. The affordable Santa Monica Boulevard spot was a hangout in the late '60s and '70s for artists like the Byrds, Alice Cooper, Elvis Costello, Janis Joplin, Bob Marley, Jim Morrison, and Warren Zevon. Tom Waits basically lived there in the 1970s. Before finding fame in Fleetwood Mac, Lindsey Buckingham and Stevie Nicks landed a recording contract while crashing at the Trop. The original Duke's Coffee Shop was within. Eating there was a rite of passage for any touring musician. It was also a short walk to Barney's Beanery, another casual haunt for the entertainment and "in" crowd. Though still possessing a certain charm, by our arrival, the 1940s-built Trop's aura was fading. In 1987, it was demolished to clear the way for a Ramada Inn.

Our rooms opened on a garden courtyard, and in true Hollywood fashion, we speedily decamped to the poolside lounge chairs. I also quickly learned that Discharge benefitted from a higher profile in Southern California than I'd experienced in other parts of the country. When a couple of groupies climbed through my bathroom window, I thought they were trying to rob me, but it turned out the band knew them. They could have just knocked.

We were now playing sold-out gigs to hundreds and even thousands of people. The biggest event on the tour was at the Grand Olympic Auditorium on the edge of downtown Los Angeles. The 10,000-capacity venue was at one time known as the "Madison Square Garden of the West." Built in 1924, it was mostly noted for putting on boxing and wrestling matches. Over the years, its notorious reputation earned it the nickname "The Bucket of Blood." From 1981 until 1986, the Olympic Auditorium hosted some of the biggest hardcore and punk shows in the world.

The night of the Olympic concert, ambulances were lined up like taxi cabs. Police helicopters hovered overhead. I was not in Buffalo anymore. Backstage, I met up-and-coming California band Suicidal Tendencies. Along with Social Distortion and MDC, they were supporting Discharge on a few of our area dates. I also was introduced to Brandon Cruz, former child actor from the television show *The Courtship of Eddie's Father* and the movie *The Bad News Bears*. He was a fixture on the Los Angeles punk scene.

What I noticed most, however, were the T-shirts worn by the audience. They were not just proclaiming allegiance to the latest punk groups—many were for heavy metal bands like Black Sabbath and Motörhead. There were handmade T-shirts too, with the word "Metallica" scrawled on them. Whatever that meant.

The concert was produced by Goldenvoice, run by Gary Tovar. The pioneering West Coast promoter was among the first to realize the marketability of punk and hardcore, and paid the musicians well. Leona told me to make sure I collected everything that was due from Tovar that evening. She had neglected to get the usual deposit from him.

I'd already had experiences with gun-flashing, knife-wielding promoters when trying to settle up at the end of the night. Early on in *this* tour, I'd decided it was best if we got paid before the band played.

The opening acts had supercharged the audience. Tovar came into our dressing room, where the guys were getting ready.

"It's time to go on," he said. I had instructed the band to wait for my signal before taking the stage. They willingly complied.

"Thanks, Gary," I said. "We'll need to get paid."

Tovar was dumbstruck. It's as if I was the first person to ever ask this of him.

He refused. Pre-recorded hardcore music echoed through the venue's sound system. Riots and stabbings were commonplace at Los Angeles hardcore and punk shows. We could hear fans shouting for the headliner. Tovar pleaded with the group, who showed remarkable resolve in supporting my plan, even though I sensed their nervousness. He relented and took me to the box office, cursing all the way.

Tovar handed me a stack of cash, shouting: "Get them on, get them on now." I stashed the money in my underwear. Viewing the sea of slam-dancing youth from my reasonably safe position behind the stage, I could feel their heat and intensity. Regardless of this seething, there were no riots.

Discharge is now credited with influencing a generation of hardcore and metal musicians, and ushering in sounds that are standard in extreme metal. Their songs have been covered by Metallica, Sepultura, Anthrax, and Machine Head.

I ended up dealing with Tovar in other roles over the next few years, as Goldenvoice grew into one of the biggest West Coast promoters. Tovar hated my guts because of that night at the Olympic, and he'd gleefully share the story with others as an example of what he perceived as my poor character. In March of 1991, he was arrested by federal agents. He'd been controlling California's largest marijuana business, and ended up spending seven years in prison for drug trafficking.

Crescent Moon and the rise of metal:

January 1984

The Discharge tour went well. My organizational abilities and management of the books pleased Leona and her Crescent Moon coworkers so much that, when we returned to the city, Leona offered me a job, as a tour coordinator. I would be securing equipment and vans, and hiring road managers. I was now earning a whopping $150 a week.

Through another member of Richard Hell's band, I scored an apartment in Soho, two blocks from the office. I moved into a 2,000-square-foot loft for $325 a month with a struggling artist as a roommate. The neighborhood, while well in transition, was still years away from becoming a gentrified, metropolitan center of art, commerce, and living. And the apartment turned out to be the least amount of money for the most space I would have in my twenty years in New York. It was incredible to be based there, and the commute was ideal.

The Prince Street Bar & Restaurant was one of my go-tos. As was Fanelli Café. My favorite nearby morning place was a personably crewed diner called Samaria. A full breakfast cost under two bucks. It was large, and never too crowded. How they paid their rent I'll never know. David Byrne, also living in the neighborhood, was a frequent customer—always alone.

Like in many other formerly "unlivable" areas, artists and musicians were the "pioneering" residents. By the mid '90s, most vestiges of old New York—sweatshops, printing presses, diners, and the original lessees—would be shoved out.

———•———

A young guy named William "Chip" Quigley financed Crescent Moon. It had been formed as a hybrid tour production/logistics company and talent booking agency.

Chip, who looked like a stoned California surfer, was the production coordinator for leading New York City concert promoter Ron Delsener, and was responsible for all the technical arrangements and crew hiring for Delsener's events.

As such, he could—and did—supply me with backstage passes to shows at Madison Square Garden. I saw everyone from Duran Duran to Yes. The Duran Duran concert was eye-opening. The audience hysteria was a first for me. The energy coming off legions of young girls shrieking, crying, and fainting before their idols reminded me of clips of the Beatles at Shea Stadium and on the Ed Sullivan show.

The media, quick to label the MTV-video driven movement of new UK bands, was calling this period "The Second British Invasion," referring to the mid-'60s influx of artists from across the pond. Duran Duran was dubbed "The Fab Five." After the performance, I made my way backstage on a wave of friends, hangers-on, and industry types. I noticed Kiss cofounder Paul Stanley hanging out. A well-dressed Simon Le Bon, Duran's lead singer, chatted with well-wishers. I availed myself of free drinks and was the last one out of the building.

With a Delsener pass, I could talk my way into any hot club in NYC. "They told me backstage to just show my badge here ..." Danceteria, Area (opened September 1983), Limelight (opened November 1983)—I had a blast discovering this new and exciting world.

Leona was very supportive, introducing me to New York and many of its urbane hotspots. She was quick to offer a compliment when I showed up sporting new apparel from Trash and Vaudeville or Canal Jean Company. It was with Leona that I had sushi for the first time; she even showed me how to use chopsticks. I was a rube no longer.

Bands signed to Crescent Moon included GBH, Peter and the Test Tube Babies, Sex Gang Children, and the Vibrators. I was thrilled to be working in the music business and in New York City, but I couldn't escape a nagging feeling. Groups that were so progressive years earlier now felt dated, as though I had already missed the peak. Leona and many of the Crescent Moon artists were at the "reflective and nostalgic" stage, talking about defunct clubs and waning or dead record deals. Tastes were changing.

Before I had a chance to contemplate this too deeply, Chip brought a new agent and partner into the agency side, now called Crescent Moon International or CMI. If your agency didn't have a three-letter acronym, you were hardly worth the paper your contracts came on. His name was Steve Martin (not the comedian), and he arrived from Magna Artists, which was shutting down.

Magna had represented hitmakers Electric Light Orchestra through much of the '70s, and Steve worked closely with a lot of college-circuit acts, like David Bromberg, Arlo Guthrie, Robert Hunter, Jorma Kaukonen, Kate & Anna McGarrigle, and Loudon Wainwright III. If I was thinking that the punk and new wave groups were sounding stale, these folks felt prehistoric. However, they toured steadily and paid the bills.

For the paunch he carried, Steve moved quickly. He would barrel into the agency each day, *Daily News* in hand, heartily acknowledging everyone individually. His prematurely graying blond hair made him seem older than he was; despite being only five or six years my senior, I was consistently greeted with, "Hello, lad." Seated next to Steve in our small open-plan office, I learned how to take care of business, including *really* booking bands. He'd set down two jumbo iced coffees, put together his call sheet, and get to work. Martin held the phone to his head like a .357 Magnum, only stopping for lunch, a meeting, or—after hanging up—to refer to some guy as "a moron." His gregarious manner and sense of humor were assets; artists, promoters, and club owners loved him. Steve Martin got things done.

Office politics arose. Chip was clearly giving Steve more of a leadership role, and while Leona *could* have worked with Steve, it became apparent that the two of them were not going to mesh.

Steve and I clicked. He liked having me around, though he wasn't fully clear on what I did. This led him to suggest I might want to earn my $150 a week by signing a few artists and booking some shows. After about eight weeks at the company, I'd just been "promoted" to agent.

———————•———————

In search of leads, I started looking through trades and fanzines. A small ad for a label called Megaforce Records, hyping a recent release by "Metallica" caught my eye. Hey! That's the name I saw scrawled on those T-shirts back on the West Coast.

Megaforce was listed as being distributed by Important Records, which had put out albums by bands already on our agency roster. I called Important, and was referred to a "Jonny Z" in New Jersey, the president of Megaforce.

I dialed the number I'd been given, and someone casually answered.

"Hi, my name is Dean Brownrout. I'm with Crescent Moon and I'm interested in speaking with Jonny Z about representing Metallica."

"This is Tony Z, I work with Jon."

"Hi Tony, I'd like to find out more about what you are doing. I was the tour manager for Discharge and—"

"You work with Discharge? They're awesome! Metallica are huge fans!"

I had Tony's attention.

With the ice broken, I learned that Megaforce—run by Jon Zazula with his wife, Marsha, and buddy Tony—had just come out with their first records, including Metallica's *Kill'Em All*. Jon and Marsha had been selling used albums at a flea market when they unearthed a cassette by Metallica through a tape trader's network. One listen to the California-cultivated band and Jon knew he had to work with them.

Jon, Tony, and Marsha had other groups on the label, including the English act Raven and NYC-based Anthrax, and were involved in what appeared to be a burgeoning underground metal movement. Their other business, "CraZed Management," managed the bands.

Professional/industry note: It is widely considered a conflict of interest for an artist's manager and record label to be one and the same, but it was hardly unusual at this nascent stage.

We set up a meeting. I plunged into the genre, listening to the Megaforce titles and other metal music.

Jon and Tony came up to the office, looking like a couple of bikers. They brought along stacks of homemade fanzines they had collected, which raved about dozens of new metal bands including the Megaforce artists.

Jon and Tony also had a bunch of issues of *Kerrang!*, a glossy, colorful UK magazine founded about three years earlier. It covered the new crop of British heavy metal and other hard rock acts from around the world, and was filled with multi-page, full-color photo spreads of the groups. Metallica appeared in recent issues.

As a teenager, I'd relied on imported British papers and magazines like *NME*, *Melody Maker*, *Sounds*, and *The Face* for trends and info. I'd continued to rely on those as a concert producer, and now as a newly minted agent.

Fans of heavy metal and hard rock in the United States were using *Kerrang!* to keep up with their favorite genre. Seeing these publications confirmed that there was a motivated and fervent fanbase for the music, and that slick publications like this could easily turn these bands into idols. Even though metal wasn't to my personal taste, I wanted in.

With Steve's support, I took on Anthrax and Raven. Anthrax had released their first album—the subtly titled *Fistful of Metal*. The album's equally subtle cover art was a grotesque illustration of someone being punched in the face with a metal-encased hand.

The Megaforce guys said they'd help organize a meeting with Metallica. They pointed out that it might be difficult to have us book the group as they were gaining some industry recognition. Other managers were interested in working with them. And, they had already secured a European tour agent. The members were recording abroad and heading to London shortly.

I convinced Steve and Leona to send me to England for the meeting—it would be my first overseas trip. Sensing I was on to a good thing, Leona insisted that she join me so she could be part of the deal.

On the Pan Am flight out of JFK, I saw the Kinks' Ray Davies. "I'm really in the music business now," I thought.

The plane was late taking off, as a heavy early-spring snow was falling. I wasn't even sure we'd be able to leave. The captain announced, "Our flight will depart as soon as they de-ice the wings again." We had stayed at the gate for too long.

After a bit, the captain came back on. "We're cleared for takeoff. With the snow, it's going to be bumpy until we get to our cruising altitude," he said, in that "I've trained for this" voice.

We headed down the runway and lifted off. The entire plane shook. We were pressed back in our seats as the plane hit an angle that was nearly vertical. I'm still an uneasy flyer; back then I was absolutely convinced we were going to crash.

Oh my god. Of course we are. Ray Davies is on the flight. Rock stars always die in plane crashes. I'm gripping the hand rest, pinned in my seat. The plane is rattling. Well, at least I'll be forever linked with Ray Davies, however brief my career in music.

The plane leveled off, and the pilot attained a smooth horizontal position above the clouds. His confident voice came on the PA again. In his affected yet somehow reassuring southern drawl, he said,

"Well, I hope you're doing well. Wanted to let y'all know we received word JFK has shut down. We were the last flight out today."

———◆———

Lying in bed that night, energized about my first visit to London, I wound down and listened to the radio. News that Marvin Gaye had been murdered by his father was flooding the airwaves.

Jonny Z had arranged for me (and Leona, of course) to meet Metallica for breakfast. The diner was in Soho, a seedy area of London soon to go through rapid transformation into a fashionable district. It was close to the Marquee Club, where the band had just performed their first UK show. (The Marquee was a prestigious music venue with an international reputation. Because of a perilously tilting façade, caused by constant music vibrations over 30 years, its Wardour Street location was condemned in 1987.)

We met the group and sat down to eat.

OK. Let's stop here for a minute. If this was a movie, the musicians and other patrons would be caught in freeze-frame; the band members and diners are variously looking out the window, at their menus, stuffing food in their mouths, and a waitress pours coffee, her arm and the liquid suspended mid-air.

I'd turn and give the following monologue directly to the camera: "Did I know these spotty-faced guys were going to become one of the biggest bands in history? No. Did they? Hell, no! Did Lars Ulrich know he'd be appearing in a Judd Apatow-produced film? Nope. Did we know we'd lose Cliff Burton less than three years later? Obviously not. (RIP, man.) We were all about 21. Metallica had played their first-ever performance in Britain *a few days earlier*. Their debut album, while doing well, had only been released in July of the previous year. Based on traditional record industry standards, when this breakfast rolled around, the band wouldn't have even been due their first royalties, if any. Sure, we all knew 'something was happening,' but hell, I'm probably just as interested in finding out what 'bangers and mash' are as I am in meeting the group."

End freeze-frame. Coffee flows, diners chat, cut to me and Leona at breakfast with … Metallica.

They were cautiously friendly. I'd gleaned from Jonny that tensions were already developing with him and the band. They still listened to him, evidenced by the fact that we were all sitting here.

The band had their next album in the can. They made it known that they were receiving music-industry interest from all quarters. They also shared that, earlier that year, their gear had been stolen in Boston. I empathized and tried to overcome their skepticism about letting us book them in the States.

Leona did her best to pitch them, but her specific experience and generational disconnect (she was nearly twenty years older) wasn't translating.

"You know, I was out on the road with Discharge a few months ago," I said. Leona had not processed the band's affinity for Discharge.

"We really like Discharge," frontman James Hetfield said. Ulrich nodded his head. We eased into a better discourse.

"Yeah, it was pretty cool seeing the reaction in LA," I said.

Being from the West Coast, they were keenly aware of what was transpiring there. We had found common ground.

Leona abruptly paid the check, said her goodbyes, and left me alone with the group. They expressed interest in touring, and we even went so far as to discuss logistics. I worked them hard, but I couldn't close the deal. We left things open. I knew enough to sense a Crescent Moon-booked tour was not imminent.

I bounded out of the diner to explore the town.

———————•———————

Upon my return to the agency, we were booking the Raven/Anthrax tour. Our understanding that we were onto something big with new metal wasn't shared by club owners and promoters across the country. Yet.

At one point, Anthrax members Scott Ian and Charlie Benante stopped by the office unannounced. Rather than wanting to discuss business, they simply wanted to meet me and have a look around.

They were very interested in the view, overlooking lower Manhattan. They stuck their heads out of an open window, assessing the scene from eight stories high. It was a gorgeous spring day. They began throwing small objects, pieces of paper, etc., out the window.

This wasn't cool. "C'mon, stop it," I said.

What they apparently heard was: "Throw the largest thing you can find out the window and see how it lands." Charlie grabbed an unopened five-gallon water cooler refill jug, and before any of us could stop him, chucked it through the window to the street below. No one was hurt.

———————•———————

This was still the early days of new metal. The fees the bands earned outside major metropolitan areas were generally between $500 and $1,500. The agency takes 10 percent. This was hardly enough to cover the overhead of an office, salaries, and expenses. Nobody was getting rich.

But I was doing fine. I had a few pairs of black jeans, a couple of button-down shirts, and could pay my rent. And the perks! Who needed actual money when you were getting free entertainment, club access with drinks, and going to catered industry parties?

We booked Raven and Anthrax a solid set of out-of-town shows in late May and early June. It was fraught from the start. Jonny Z sent them out underfunded. Make that *un*funded. I received a call from Jon almost the minute the bands arrived at their first gig. He told me that they were stuck in a Midwest parking lot, hungry and out of gas. They couldn't afford to continue. Seriously? They're already out of money? The "tour" was only one week long!

Faced with canceling the dates and jeopardizing our relationships with both the groups and the promoters, Steve uneasily loaned them the considerable sum of $5,000, figuring he could at least recoup some of the advance from the promoters' deposits. We also had both bands booked for a West Coast run at the top of the summer, from which he could draw funds.

Jonny was desperate, and promised to pay back any shortfall. He never did. We lost money on these guys from the get-go. And Jon would spin things to his advantage, blaming the agency for what was, in reality, a great bunch of bookings and a really generous act on Steve's part.

———•———

Having yet to find a new circle of friends or dates, from time to time I relied on inviting women from my hometown to join me in NYC.

One such visitor from the homeland arrived. We spent the day enjoying the sights, seeing some bands, and drinking. And drinking. Last call. The clock hit 4 a.m. (!). Much too early to call it a night, I thought. Ah, the energy of youth. I need a nap just recalling these types of events.

Though I had never actually been to one, I'd heard about unlicensed after-hours clubs scattered through Alphabet City, like Save the Robots and Lucky Seven. The area, on the Lower East Side between Avenues A and D, was then a hub of drug activity, gangs, squatters, and street people. Government and police efforts to quash these conditions, as well as encroaching gentrification would result in riots over the next few years. Avenue A was as far east as I would usually venture.

"Let's go to an after-hours club," 4-a.m., gin-soaked me said to my companion, as if I did this all the time.

We grabbed a cab and headed to the randomly selected intersection of Avenue B and 6th Street. Somewhere along B, among the abandoned and burnt-out buildings, I saw a tall Black guy walking south, the only person visible in any direction. I asked the driver to stop and we got out. "Hey, hi," I yelled to the man, who had already noticed us stopping and had seemingly slowed his gait.

My date and I hustled across the street. "Do you know where there are any after-hours clubs around here?"

"Oh, sure," he said, as if he'd been walking by for this sole purpose. "Follow me."

I'm making chirpy small talk. Broken glass, baggies, and an occasional syringe litter the curb. Is that blood? Nah. Part of me is thinking, "What the hell did I just do?" Though somehow (likely the liquor and the early morning hour), I felt we were in capable hands and not being led to an alley to be mugged—or worse.

Our new friend took us around the corner to a heavy unmarked door, and knocked. A rectangular peephole opens, barely revealing two eyes. "They're OK," our guide says. After a slight hesitation, the door swings open. I shake hands with our chaperone and thank him. For a small fee, we're asked to join this "members-only club"— either some kind of dodge to get past the liquor laws or a way to ensure easier access in the future. We're handed a membership card. Like I'd be able to find this place again.

Entering the murky space, we grab a seat. A small crowd is partying. Men, women, gay, straight, cross-dressers. I spot Keith Haring. There is a great vibe. We settle in for more drinking. The club continues to fill up. Some time later we decide to call it a night. We walk downtown, aiming for Soho, half-looking for a cab. I turn to my date and, as the sun was rising, we lock eyes. Amid the quiet, empty streets, we kiss.

———————•———————

I turned my focus to Metallica. Larger record companies had become aware of the band's growing popularity, record sales, and positive press. Jonny Z and the musicians were hungry for the group to be seen in New York City for precisely that reason. While I had no illusions we would work with them after more influential managers, labels, and agents got involved, I agreed to set up a showcase.

We added Metallica to the roster—however briefly. Steve and I convinced well-known tri-state promoter John Scher that a Raven/Metallica/Anthrax bill could work at Roseland Ballroom, a 3,500-capacity venue in the heart of Manhattan. Scher booked the event, but he and his staff remained skeptical that these three fairly unknown bands meant anything in ticket sales.

(Scher still holds the record for the largest-ever concert held in New Jersey—125,000 people attended his 1977 presentation of the Grateful Dead at Raceway Park. He is also one of the unrepentant promoters of Woodstock '99, which is documented as one of the most catastrophic large-scale music festivals of the twentieth century.)

By July, Leona left the agency, and Chip was out. Steve took over. Years later, Chip would successfully manage the band Sugar Ray. Another agent, Elizabeth Rush was brought in; her artists included such well-respected acts as Van Dyke Parks, the Roches, and Richard Thompson.

I appreciated Leona giving me my first big-city show business "break" and was grateful for all she had done for me in such a short time. As I would come to learn, friends, associates, and acquaintances in such a striving and mercurial field can be fleeting. Leona continued booking heavy metal bands on her own for a few more years before moving into New Jersey real estate sales.

With all these changes, and new clients, Steve purchased a large ad in one of the trades, listing our combined roster. At the bottom of the ad, our names—mine, his, and Elizabeth Rush's—appeared in the same type size.

Unbeknownst to her, I overheard Rush voicing her displeasure on the phone. "I can't believe mine and my artists' names are listed alongside this 'Dean Brownrout' and horrid little bands like Metallica."

On July 27, Metallica released *Ride the Lightning* on Megaforce Records in the US.

Our August 3, 1984, Roseland show, billed as "A Midsummer's Night Scream," sold out and became a legendary event in Metallica's and Anthrax's histories and, indeed, in metal music lore.

In recent years, Roseland had begun to acquire a reputation as a dangerous place. Early '80s disco nights drew a crowd that the neighbors didn't love. But the owners and promoter had never seen a crowd *like this* before. Testosterone- and liquor-fueled youth, freed from their parents' yoke, were puking in the bathroom—if they made it that far. Couples had sex in plain view. Metal and glass ornamentation ringing the venue was punched or kicked into ribbons and shards. The concert made money for Scher, though his take was diminished since he had to reimburse Roseland for the damage inflicted by the "exuberant" audience.

It was a coming-out party for independent metal bands in America. All three groups were offered major-label contracts shortly thereafter. Metallica was on its journey to something un-precedented, and I wouldn't be part of that. Still, from that point forward, I was constantly approached by other emerging metal acts seeking an agent. The quick reputation earned while working with Raven, Anthrax, Metallica, and the Roseland show gave me access to a crop of rising metal talent. I'd earned a rep as the "new metal guy" in the agency business.

———•———

I connected with Richard Sanders, who was booking a 1,500-2,000-person capacity Brooklyn rock club called "L'Amour." The former disco was in Bay Ridge, around the corner from "2001 Odyssey," the spot made famous in the 1977 film *Saturday Night Fever*. Touted as the "Rock Capital of Brooklyn" ("Capitol" was misspelled on its awning) and usually referred to as "La-Morz" by the locals, it was the East Coast nexus for heavy metal music.

Groups like Accept, Fastway, King Diamond, Quiet Riot, Ratt, Twisted Sister, and Y&T came through L'Amour in the early days.

And, of course, Anthrax, Overkill, Metallica, and other newcomers. Between sets, a DJ discerningly pumped out the latest European and US metal releases through the club's 50,000-watt sound system, including frequent first-plays for unknown bands' demo tapes. A large screen showed in-house-made videos of horror movie scenes spliced to sync with the recorded music, which was quite progressive. W.A.S.P.'s "Animal (F**k Like a Beast)" was combined with clips from porn star John Holmes' highlight reel.

Richard and I had a great rapport. We were both music-biz professionals who could work in any genre, regardless of our taste. He had a droll sense of humor, and was easy to communicate with.

"Richard, I've been approached by this band Loudness from Japan …"

"I'll pay them $10,000 for a weekend at the club."

"Richard, I'm booking a band named—"

"I'll pay you $5,000 for a show with the band."

Pretty soon Richard was placing orders with me. "Can you get …?" I could wrap an entire tour around a L'Amour gig. Often an act would come from out of town just to play the venue. Fans flocked to the place.

———•———

Near the end of year, Steve took me aside. "Dean, money here is getting tight. I wanted to give you a heads up. There might be some weeks where payroll is delayed."

In Steve's mind, this was code for: "I'm trusting you with this information; can we work together as a team and try to 'entrepreneurially' get past this?"

And, what *I* heard was: "We don't have any money to pay you. You're going to be fired soon."

I found a new agency job within three days, for 100 bucks more a week, and gave notice. Steve was happy for me, but apparently surprised. He explained what he had really meant. He had hoped I would stay with him. I really liked and respected Steve, but I needed to know I was going to be paid.

———•———

Steve changed the agency name to Music Business Agency ("MBA"). Near the end of the decade, he sold it to the William Morris Agency ("WMA"), where he became one of its key booking agents, signing Barenaked Ladies and Crash Test Dummies, among others. A few years later, Martin left to spearhead the new New York office of The Agency Group ("TAG"), a UK-based agency that was setting up a US operation. There, over the course of twenty years, he was instrumental in growing the company into a worldwide power with over forty agents in the US and a roster of hundreds of acts. His personal book included Bruce Cockburn, Bob Geldof, David Gilmour, Dolly Parton, Scorpions, and Brian Wilson. In 2008, Martin was awarded "Agent of the Year" by concert industry publication *Pollstar*. After a successful follow-up working with the Agency for the Performing Arts ("APA"), he ditched the acronyms and opened Paladin Artists in 2021. As testament to Steve's character and ability, nearly 40 years later he still represents many of his Crescent Moon artists.

TRA and moving up (Arriba!): 1985

I started work at the recently formed Talent Resource Agency (TRA), founded by agent Arne Brogger. The Minnesota transplant was almost too decent to be in the music business; he didn't stay in it for much longer. His exacting standards and corporate demeanor made some of the industry's more shambolic elements difficult for him to handle.

Arne previously was an agent at Variety Artists in Minneapolis. The booking agency counted John Prine and Pure Prairie League among its more prominent clients. In the lobby of the Midwest firm hung a photo of their late colleague, Kenneth Cortese, who perished in a 1973 Louisiana plane crash with singer-songwriter Jim Croce. Arne was responsible for bringing then little-known blues guitarist Stevie Ray Vaughan into Variety. Arne begged promoters to book Vaughan for $200 a night, juicing the gigs with a contractual caveat that, if they didn't like his performance, they didn't have to pay him. Frustrated with Variety's disinterest in Vaughan and other artists of his, Arne hopped on a plane to New York City and started Talent Resource Agency, bringing with him a formidable list of actively touring blues musicians, including Albert Collins, Son Seals, and Koko Taylor. Many of them were associated with Chicago-based Alligator Records.

Our offices were located in a converted apartment building on 54th and Seventh, around the corner from the Carnegie Deli. The area is a historical center of the entertainment industry in New

York, and a hotbed of television and recording studios, record labels, agencies, and the like.

Robert Singerman, a pioneering manager and agent in the late '70s/early '80s new wave scene, had an arm's-length financial interest in the agency as well as keeping an office there. Singerman had recently gone through a tough breakup with longtime business partner and close friend, Frank Riley. He had moved his operation out of the Cable Building and was finding his feet again. Robert recommended me to Arne and encouraged me to join them.

In one capacity or another, Singerman had represented 10,000 Maniacs, the Fleshtones, R.E.M., the Smithereens, and Violent Femmes, among many others. My relationship with him dated back to Buffalo, when I booked many of his bands. He was actually the guy who sold me the Nico show and had surrendered to my imploring.

On the TRA roster when I joined was New York folk artist Suzanne Vega. The unsigned performer had been attracting local notice for a few years; Arne recognized her promise early on. He developed a relationship with Vega and her manager, Ron Fierstein (brother of actor/playwright Harvey Fierstein). Arne began booking her gigs around the country, even putting her up at his mom's house when she played Minneapolis. As is industry practice, contracts had been delivered to Vega to formalize her relationship with us. Meanwhile, an article about Vega in the *New York Times* caught David Geffen's eye, who then flew into town to see her. Geffen's interest sparked a bidding war, and Vega ended up signing with A&M Records. Vega didn't sign with us as her agency, and the final phone "conversation" between Fierstein and Arne was memorable. Arne uncharacteristically lost his cool—he took it personally. Everyone in the building heard him yell, "Fuck you, Ron," and slam the phone down. I wasn't surprised to see her go.

Acts booked by TRA also included Afrika Bambaataa, John Cale, the Jim Carroll Band, the dB's, Richard Hell, and Jeffrey Lee Pierce (of the Gun Club). All these artists were fed to the agency by Singerman.

The other agent in the small firm was Andy Somers, a fired refugee from the William Morris Agency mailroom. He was the archetypal salesman, whose practiced glibness and ability to pitch a band or a show made him reliable, but I could always see his wheels turning, planning his next move.

Andy had a few local groups who didn't generate hefty fees. He still delivered for them, but God forbid they needed him on a Thursday afternoon or evening. At those times, all his energies were poured into securing the appropriate food and drink, and being home, in front of his TV, to watch Tom Selleck in *Magnum, P.I.*—while it had been a top-rated show, its moment was fading. But Andy was a #1 fan for sure.

Arne's brother Ivar, who would become a recognizable film and television character actor, stopped by the office from time to time. One of his recent roles had been in the camp horror/sci-fi film *C.H.U.D.*—which, you should know if you don't, stands for Cannibalistic Humanoid Underground Dwellers, and is a great general insult for any … chuds, who I regularly came across in the music business. Andy took to yelling "CHUD!" every time he spotted Ivar.

Andy and Arne gobbled up my stories of the metal world. As agents, they already knew there was a growing market for this sound. Arne had hired me to help disseminate it for them.

In many instances, Andy, Arne, and I worked together to sign artists to the agency. We would identify the groups and target the musicians, their managers, attorneys, and labels to bring an act into the fold.

We added the veteran English extreme metal band Venom, a major influence on the "thrash" genre, as this new metal sound was being called. Slayer, out of California, influenced by Venom, joined us as well.

Like many others following the music, I'd recognized a group called Megadeth as the next potential breakout. Megadeth was formed by Dave Mustaine, a talented metal guitarist and songwriter, who had been in an early version of Metallica. Before they'd

even hit the small big-time, Metallica had kicked him out for attitude problems.

Now, as Metallica started its rise to world domination, fanzines
were running interviews with Mustaine. He had an axe to grind
and something to prove.

Megadeth's demo tape was widely circulated. It showed promise, and made apparent that a band including Mustaine could be
marketable. Several indie metal labels were interested. They signed
with Combat Records, an in-house label of Important Records
(also home to Megaforce). Their first release was coming out in the
summer. We began working with them.

Somers—no fool and ever the quick study—had also taken to
bringing in some of the newer metal acts on his own.

My booking territory encompassed the West Coast (plus
L'Amour in Brooklyn; I had a good thing going there!), which
included dealing with promoters Goldenvoice and Bill Graham
Presents. It was an epicenter for emerging metal, so it made sense.
Plus, it suited my hours. Doing business with "the Coast," I didn't
have to get in too early.

———————•———————

TRA shared the office with an entertainment attorney named Jules
Kurz, and his faithful secretary, Shirley.

Jules had a few gold records on the wall, attesting to his earlier triumphs. He was a likable guy who had negotiated contracts
for Ozzy Osbourne and Bruce Springsteen, and briefly managed
Grace Jones. Now he seemed to be losing more business than he
was keeping. And he really savored his three-martini lunches.

Shirley was an older woman with a huge appetite for meatball
subs; she ate one drowning in red sauce every day. She was also
known for her diligence and lack of humor.

Given the layout of the place, my desk was in what would have
been the living room, along with Shirley and our assistant, Anne
Katzenbach. Anne's father, Nicholas deBelleville Katzenbach, had

an illustrious resume. He was a deputy attorney general under Bobby Kennedy, an attorney general under Lyndon Johnson, and counsel to IBM. As a city kid, passionate about music, she followed and participated in all the latest music scenes. She was there for the emergence of punk and new wave at CBGB and the Mudd Club, discoed at Studio 54, and connected with the avant-garde no wave community at White Columns. During her time at TRA, she was hanging out at the Dive, a club devoted to reimagining the 1960s do-it-yourself garage rock ethos. Somers called her "the bohemian debutante."

Jules left Shirley a Dictaphone tape each night—letters and legal documents—for her to type up the next day. As I came to know and dislike Shirley, I enjoyed substituting the latest Megadeth, Slayer, or Venom cassette for Jules' dictation. She didn't take kindly to it, though Anne and I found it reliably amusing.

———•———

I settled into my job and my life in the city. I made a friend who was the bartender at a Mexican eatery called Arriba Arriba. It was a short walk from the office, at 51st and 9th, on the seedy western edge of the theater district.

The neighborhood was the gritty Hell's Kitchen, and the restaurant was more upmarket than many other local establishments. A few blocks southeast, Times Square was not the family-friendly place it is today. Arriba Arriba became my unofficial second office. Friends and associates knew it was my post-work spot, if they needed to get in touch with me.

The tight bar had half a dozen seats, and standing room for a dozen at most. That made meeting new people a cinch. The crowd was diverse. Many New York City adventures—both prurient and chaste—began with a visit there.

Downtown, another Mexican-themed restaurant and bar, Bandito, between 9th and 10th streets on Second Avenue, served as my closer-to-home base of operations.

It was a prime example of 1980s *Miami Vice*-meets-MTV restaurant design. Heavy application of black and white tiling and neon lights were evident. Its dual Taylor frozen margarita machine was in constant use. The food was … edible. Between Bandito and Arriba Arriba, I developed a lifelong love of tequila.

Everyone who worked at Bandito was a musician, actor, or aspiring something. The ownership capitalized on the hip locale, and ran ads in Andy Warhol's *Interview* magazine. Customers came from the worlds of art, music, and modeling. I once saw Christie Brinkley. She nibbled on the corner of a tortilla chip, and then set it down—stuffed! Diana Ross stopped by, as did Rolling Stone Bill Wyman.

Still, it was an unpretentious destination open to all who could find a chair. There were about forty seats in the dining area, and room at the bar for twelve. It helped to know Dieter Runge, the night manager.

At Bandito, my drinking pals included two husband-and-wife duos: Ivan Julian and Cynthia Sley—he was one of Richard Hell and the Voidoids' original guitarists and still played with Hell occasionally, and she was in the Bush Tetras—and Fred Smith and Jan Mullen; Fred had been in Television. I'd become friendly with Ivan back in Buffalo when I booked his band, the Outsets. He was one of the first people to welcome me to New York City. A decade or more older than me on average, the quartet made up New York rock royalty. They'd been there at the start of the new wave and punk music movements at seminal joints like CBGB, Hurrah, and the Mudd Club. I hung on their stories.

I ran into Adam Yauch from the Beastie Boys there once. I knew him well enough to have a casual chat. I'd met him hanging out at the ZE Records office around the corner from TRA. ZE was putting out our agency client John Cale's records. Yauch's band was making a name for themselves, but hadn't released their breakout first album, *Licensed to Ill*.

I invited a girl from Buffalo down to visit me. A tall, gorgeous brunette, I took her to my various hangouts when she arrived.

Marylou's, an upscale Italian restaurant on West 9th, was our first stop. The slightly disreputable venue, located half a floor below street level, attracted a mix of gangsters, actors, authors, and other New York City nightlifers. (Jay McInerney based the fictional "Evelyn's" on the place in his novel *The Good Life*.) Its high-energy atmosphere was definitely bolstered by the cocaine flowing in the bathrooms. It habitually stayed open well after closing hour.

We grabbed seats at the bar. Martino, the long-time bartender and keeper of many secrets, served us. James Belushi was hanging out. Martino was quick to offer the actor praise as he muddled his drink. "I really liked you in *Thief.* That was a good movie," he said, referring to director Michael Mann's 1981 neo-noir theatrical debut. When Daryl Hall, then an MTV staple and bona fide star, stepped up to the bar, my friend was astounded. Just another day in my new life.

We headed further downtown, to a Tribeca loft party. Less than five minutes after we arrived, all three of the Beastie Boys surrounded us. I knew it wasn't their enthusiasm for my attention that had them beeline our way, but rather the allure of my beautiful friend.

The three young guys went into a shtick to gain her interest, riffing through their routine. In faux British accents, they put on what amounted to a song-and-dance act. She smiled and laughed, but they soon realized they were getting nowhere.

Licensed to Ill dropped the following year, and became the first rap LP to top the *Billboard* album charts. It was the fastest-selling album ever for Columbia. The Beasties made the cover of every major music magazine, and their videos were in constant rotation.

Decades later, I ran into the brunette beauty, back in Buffalo, where she still resided. She reminded me of that night. The story of our meeting the Beastie Boys in Tribeca had become part of her personal history and a tale she kept in her raconteur's arsenal.

———•———

The office doorbell rang. I opened it to find model and singer Grace Jones, imperious-looking in her head wrap, scarf, and sunglasses.

"Excuse me … is Jules in?" she asked, enunciating each word in a most proper-sounding British-Jamaican accent. I asked her to come in and Shirley immediately ushered her back to see Jules.

Much to everyone's embarrassment, the sounds of their not-happy "discussion" started spilling out.

"Where the hell have you been?" Jules shouted.

"How could you sign that without consulting me?" Jones screamed.

It went on like this for ten minutes. When Jules' door opened, we tried to look busy.

Jones stomped to the front door, opened it and dramatically announced: "I'm very sorry, people, to have disrupted your day … but I'm having my period." And with that she swiveled, threw her scarf over her shoulder, and left.

———•———

On July 11, 1985, Arne told me Alligator Records chief Bruce Iglauer had called him. Iglauer conveyed that Alligator artist Lonnie Mack was expecting the Rolling Stones' Ron Wood to show up at his gig that evening.

Mack was in town for two nights at the Lone Star Café on Fifth Avenue, an intimate space with a pleasantly gritty atmosphere that belied its tony address; it offered a range of acts and was a great place to see performers.

Mack was a blues-rocker, a musician's musician, not widely popular, but deeply admired by peers and those in the know. He had resurfaced after a decade, and was playing out on the strength of his successful new recording.

At the club the previous evening, Wood had stopped by. There, he told Mack he would come back for Mack's second appearance the next night—and that he might bring bandmate, Keith Richards, with him. Maybe they'd sit in during the set.

I secured a place on the guest list for me and a pal. The chance to be this close to even two of the Stones on stage was exciting. I called my old employer Steve Martin, to share the good word. He had other plans, but made it his business to tell his client, actress-comedian Sandra Bernhard.

Cut to that night. My friend and I got to the Lone Star. It was practically empty. Was this a ruse? This kind of news—that Keith Richards and Ron Wood were going to perform a "surprise" show in a New York City club—hardly stays secret for long, especially among music industry insiders. (*Everyone* knew Prince was going to appear with protégé Sheila E. at the Ritz, a 2,500-capacity club, the previous September.)

Bernhard showed up, accompanied by actor Matt Dillon, a regular on the New York club scene and an in-demand rising star. They hung about near the front of the stage. I was thinking what Steve might say if she reported the evening was a dud.

My plus-one was Alan Donatelli. Originally from Buffalo, he'd moved to the city the same time I did. I frequently hired him to road-manage tours for some of my more "difficult" bands, like the bickering UK Subs, the heroin-addled yet gifted Jeffrey Lee Pierce of the Gun Club, and punk hotel-room-wreckers the Exploited. Alan could handle himself and knew his way around clubs and concert venues.

Ever thirsty, Alan wandered backstage, where he found no people and a cooler full of frosty beers. He grabbed a few and met me back out front. We waited … and waited some more. No Keef. We headed toward the back of the club, where there was a side door. We figured we'd slip out, and call it a night.

As we went up the dark hall, I heard pounding on the door. More pounding. We're thinking of leaving anyway, so what's the harm in opening it? Probably a locked-out staffer.

I pushed it open, and beheld Keith Richards and Ron Wood.

"Oh, hi … come in," I stammered, forgetting to act cool. "Oh, hi." Jeez.

I held the door as a single file of true rock royalty followed after Wood and Richards, each one greeting me kindly: Mick Jagger, Bob Dylan, U2/Stones producer Steve Lillywhite, and an entourage. Adrian Belew (King Crimson) and Paul Simon brought up the rear.

With this development, we decided to stick around. Alan bolted to the second-floor dressing room to grab more "complimentary" beers, while the new arrivals settled in throughout the club—which strangely still wasn't filling up much.

Alan came back. "I was trying to open a beer on the edge of the urinal. It sprayed all over, and got the guy next to me—it was Keith."

"What did he say?" I asked.

"He said, 'Oi, mate! What the hell ya' doing!?'"

Mack got the crowd going. The club was still navigable, and we easily maneuvered closer to the stage. Wood and Richards joined Mack onstage for the promised jam. The three traded licks on a rocker and a blues number.

Jagger and Dylan watched from the balcony. This was the kind of thing I'd read about in *Rolling Stone* as a teenager, and here I was less than two years into my New York adventure. I knew it was special, and I was feeling pretty good.

(When Lonnie Mack passed away in 2016, Belew, who had been in the city recording *Graceland* with Simon back then, recalled the evening in a memorial Facebook post: "Paul [Simon] and I went to the Lone Star Café to see Lonnie play ... Paul introduced me to Bob Dylan, hiding in the balcony stairwell ... After the show Paul and I went backstage. There sat Lonnie with Keith and Mick. In his southern drawl, [Lonnie] was extolling the virtues of fishing in Indiana where he lived. He turned and saw me, interrupted his own story, and said, 'Hey Adrin! Still playin' with that King Crizmun?'")

Richards, Wood, and Dylan made their way to Philadelphia that weekend. On July 13, 1985, they performed together at the celebrated Live Aid concert in front of 100,000 people at John F. Kennedy Stadium.

Jagger also played Live Aid. He did a five-song set with Hall and Oates as his backup band. Tina Turner joined him. The huge fundraiser was broadcast around the globe to over one billion viewers in 110 countries.

———•———

Our office assistant, Anne Katzenbach, left. To replace her, we hired Marci Weber, a classic New York character. She'd drag in late every morning, which drove Arne crazy. Sunglasses hid her bloodshot eyes and club-hopping hangover—if you've seen the British comedy *Absolutely Fabulous,* you have a visual for her persona.

Marci previously worked for a high-profile music agent who had recently died of complications from drug and alcohol abuse. Her dad had also been in show business, representing the frenetic comedian Charlie Callas.

A certified Anglophile, every story of hers began with, "Colin said …" or, "Then Nigel …" Back then, every British musician was named Colin or Nigel, so we never knew which one she was referring to. This made her easy to tease. All we had to say was, "Oh my god, wait till Nigel hears about this!"

When it was time to work though—usually around noon—she'd kick into gear. She was laser-focused, generating contracts and locking in concerts with efficient intensity.

Marci and I got along well; she made me laugh. We'd go out for dinner and drinks after work. Marci's go-to was a casual restaurant called Columbus, on, you guessed it, Columbus Avenue (at 69th Street). It was a known actors' hangout. Another of her predilections was proximity to celebrities, which along with her sometimes impish sense of humor, could result in awkward situations.

The place was owned by several people in the arts and entertainment business, including actor Paul Herman and dancer Mikhail Baryshnikov. Regulars at Columbus included Warren Beatty, Michael Keaton, Anjelica Huston, and New York guys like Robert De Niro, Danny Aiello, and Christopher Walken.

Once, as we were ensconced at a table in the Columbus dining room, Marci initiated a conversation about it-couple Sean Penn and Madonna. Taking her cue, I readily replied with something I'd recently read. Rather than continue on the topic *she* had started, she shushed me and pointed to the couple in question one table over. Like I said, impish.

Marci was as ambitious as I was, and had her eye on becoming a manager. We decided to collaborate on an outside project, partnering to pursue a new British band called Chiefs of Relief—their experimental sound combined hip-hop, punk, and electronic. Marci had an in with the group, which featured the Sex Pistols' Paul Cook and Matthew Ashman from Bow Wow Wow. I had a management contract drawn up and bought a ticket for Marci to fly to London. She was unable to land the artist.

She did achieve her goals, managing Richard Melville Hall, better known as Moby, in the 1990s. By the end of that decade, Moby had sold 20 million records worldwide, and is still considered one of the most important dance figures of his time. I guess those late nights of clubbing paid off for Marci.

———•———

I had formed a close working relationship with a street-hustling concert promoter named Chris Williamson, a long-haired Juilliard drop-out who had worked at the storied club Studio 54. He lived on a houseboat at the 79th Street Boat Basin, the only marina with year-round residency in New York City.

Under the banner Rock Hotel, Chris had been putting on well-attended hardcore punk shows with bands like Bad Brains, Cro-Mags, Kraut, and Murphy's Law. The venue was in the ballroom of the Jane West, a seedy old hotel on Manhattan's lower west side.

The building was opened in 1908 by the American Seamen's Friend Society, opposite the Cunard Line pier, to provide housing for sailors passing through the port of New York. The organization ventured to bring respite from the transient lodging choices sailors generally found in their travels. In 1912, *RMS Titanic* crew survivors were brought to the hotel for comfort and prayer.

Around the middle of the century, the place was used as subsidized housing for drug addicts and those down on their luck. Its sordid reputation continued for another couple decades after the Rock Hotel era. *Hedwig and the Angry Inch*, the musical co-written by and starring John Cameron Mitchell, debuted there in 1998. Mitchell, speaking with *Rolling Stone*, recalled a body bag containing an overdose victim being wheeled through the lobby, past audience members waiting to get in. The site was designated a New York City landmark in 2000. In 2008, new owners took over; they removed the bulletproof glass from the lobby, among other refurbishments, and it became one of the hottest celebrity party spots in the city.

When things at the Jane West looked untenable for Chris' shows—mostly owing to neighborhood disruption—I introduced him to Joe Plotkin of John Scher's production company. Plotkin was booking the Ritz, in lower New York.

Even though it was unusual for another promoter to be allowed to use it, I encouraged Joe to let Chris promote concerts at the Ritz. After all, Plotkin could reason, what do I need Chris for when I can book these bands myself? I persuaded Joe that having the Rock Hotel imprimatur and Chris' guerilla marketing abilities would be a boon. Plotkin relented, though he asked me if the guy had something on me.

He paid Chris fifty cents a head for promoting and managing the Rock Hotel series at the Ritz. With powerful and creative lineups that included Agnostic Front, Circle Jerks, D.O.A., Motörhead, Ramones, and Wendy O. Williams, it was a huge success. Chris appeared in a widely circulated Miller beer magazine ad, featuring him sitting on a road case "after a gig" enjoying a cold beer. The caption read: "Wrapping it up at the Rock Hotel, New York, NY."

I booked Slayer into L'Amour in Brooklyn. The band was signed to Los Angeles-based Metal Blade Records. The label's president, Brian Slagel, was a pioneering figure in new metal, and was coming to town to see them play. The young Slagel was responsible for releasing the first commercial recording of Metallica, Ratt, and others on his compilation album *The New Heavy Metal Revue Presents Metal Massacre.*

Somers and I decided to give Slagel the "VIP agency treatment"—we didn't think he'd ever experienced our brand of NYC over-the-top hospitality. Our plan to impress Slagel had the ulterior motive of inspiring him to recommend more of his label's bands to join our agency roster.

We arranged for a full-length "rock star limo"—well, *Somers* arranged—to drive us to dinner and then out to L'Amour to see Slayer.

Somers had mentioned he "had contacts in the limousine business," and revealed that he'd sometimes worked as a limo driver prior to joining TRA. On the night of the show, Andy and I waited outside the office for the car before picking up Slagel at his hotel.

I could have died when, instead of the slick *black* limo I'd assumed Somers had booked, it was a *white* "prom/wedding" limousine. I was mortified. Slinking into the back seat, I could barely contain my displeasure with Andy.

However, when the T-shirt clad Slagel climbed in, he was excited. He'd never ridden in a limo before. Still, I anticipated the haranguing the fans would heap on us, as they waited to see this extreme thrash band—and we arrive in the most punk-ass ride on the planet.

When we pulled up to L'Amour, I shot out of the car as fast as I could. To my surprise, the crowd outside was murmuring approvingly. When Slagel emerged, they went nuts. He was already an icon.

Those who recognized him from metal magazines and fanzines shouted "Slagel!" Those who only knew him by name quickly learned who the man clambering out of the formal limo was. They also shouted their approval. Word spread throughout the club that Brian Slagel had arrived in a limousine.

Slagel was thrilled with the evening and did, in fact, recommend more artists to us.

Over the decades, in accounts about the early days of Slayer, L'Amour, Slagel or the history of new metal, the story of the white limo carrying him to that show is frequently referred to. I'm still embarrassed.

———•———

David Wolin, an acquaintance from Buffalo, called me at TRA. A drummer, still in his late teens, he'd formed a garage rock band called the Splatcats and was looking for an agent. After hearing their self-released EP, I booked a show or two for them in New York. While they were in the city, Wolin arranged for a live radio interview with WNYU. I was impressed with his resourcefulness.

I tuned in to the broadcast and fell out of my seat laughing at the humor and shared sensibility the young group displayed. Their club show was great. I invited them to the office and dinner, agreeing to permanently add them to the roster.

Within days, David called to say they had been offered a deal with Celluloid Records, a New York label. A friend of theirs from back home, former college radio DJ Howard Enis, was working in sales at Celluloid. (Howard went by his on-air name, Cal Zone.) Cal introduced the Splatcats to the label head and persuaded him to sign them. This seemed like, and would prove to be, a great entrée for me into the record world.

I told David I also wanted to manage them. They went for it. Managing bands at TRA was still outside my job description as an agent, but my professional gaze was continuing to look outward.

———•———

We brought former New York Dolls guitarist Johnny Thunders into the agency. The often charming but infamously fucked-up and heroin-addicted rocker was unreliable and had a reputation for not showing up at gigs, or if he did, being unable to perform. We knew what we were getting into, but chose to work with him anyhow.

After an entire US tour was booked, Thunders' people advised me he had "crushed his hand in a car door," and it was postponed. (He made good on the dates the following spring.)

———————•———————

Through 1985, metal continued to grow in popularity. Metallica led the way, kicking down doors for others to follow. The band was booked to headline a New Year's Eve concert for promoter Bill Graham on December 31, 1985, at the 8,500-capacity San Francisco Civic Auditorium. (When the celebrated music impresario died in a helicopter crash in 1991, the venue was renamed the Bill Graham Civic Auditorium.)

The Graham organization controlled the Bay Area concert market. They made life easy for me. I could usually book at least three well-paid club dates for an artist with one phone call to them. As one of the region's (and country's) most prominent promoters, his company also had a lock on the larger SF venues, enabling me to get our bands added as support in those types of gigs.

I had arranged for a couple of our groups, including Megadeth, to open for Metallica that New Year's, and flew out to represent the agency at the event. Tom Araya from Slayer was hanging out backstage. Michael Alago (the A&R guy who signed Metallica to Elektra Records) was theoretically in attendance. I saw him just as he passed out in a dressing room. Michael missed the chance to fully ring in the New Year, but I think he was having a good time anyway. As always, Dave Mustaine (leader of Megadeth, formerly of Metallica, in case you forgot) was bitching about something—possibly his band's position as the opener: fourth on the four-act bill.

Checking into, and out of, Rock Hotel: 1986

As a student of music business history, I'd devoured books and stories on the subject since childhood. In addition to Ertegun and Geffen, I admired record industry figures like Neil Bogart (Casablanca), Jac Holzman (Elektra), and Chris Blackwell (Island).

I was restless. I was growing tired of being a "ten-percenter," and of getting the blame for things, which, at the club-booking level, is regularly laid at the feet of the agent—no matter what the problem. Canceling on promoters is a horrible feeling. And I'd just had two tours drop out, first with Thunders and then UK goth rockers Alien Sex Fiend, who backed out of a beautifully booked North American set of dates. Then there's the 2 a.m. phone calls from artists about something you generally can't fix: meal issues, disputed ticket sales, "drum riser politics," or having to deal with the fallout of Dave Mustaine slicing his guitar through a 30-foot-high video screen at the Ritz. It was galling, especially when it came from sources like Megadeth, well before it may have been justified by the band's eventual gold and platinum records. Too much junkie business.

In my youthful impatience and frustration, I told Arne and Andy that I never wanted to speak with Mustaine again. The metal guitarist had worn on my last nerve. If I was going to deal with this type of thing, I wanted to get paid. I started looking with envy to the record company side of things. (Andy immediately got on the phone with Mustaine and began calling him every day, even if only to talk about the weather. He established a long-term personal and professional relationship with the band.)

———————•———————

A lot of fresh New York City talent—a new wave of hardcore bands with a similar energy and appeal as the current crop of metal bands I was working with—was introduced and gained exposure at the Rock Hotel shows. That meant lots of record companies sniffing around. One of them, Profile Records, was on top of the charts with Run-DMC. They approached Chris Williamson regarding the Cro-Mags, a promising group of his.

Williamson sought my counsel many times, asking how to handle bands, agents, politics, and the like. I related to his entrepreneurial nature—with my concert promotion and production background, I understood both the challenges and opportunities he encountered. And he commented that my deliberate and thoughtful advice had a calming effect on his own admittedly anxious and edgy personality.

He called me from a payphone after he met with Profile.

"Dean, Profile made me an offer for the Cro-Mags."

"That's fantastic, Chris," I said.

"I don't know if I want to sign them to Profile—it's a rap label. What do they know about promoting rock, especially hardcore?"

Without missing a beat I said: "Why don't you go back to them and say you want to start Rock Hotel Records? You can sign the Cro-Mags and some other bands and keep control of the marketing. You can teach them how to sell these groups just like you've taught them over at the Ritz."

I could hear his jaw drop. "Wow. What a great idea!" Before I could manage another thought, he said, "I'll call you back!" And hung up.

Later that day Chris called with the report.

"They agreed!" he said. "They're moving into new offices and they think this would be a perfect way to get a rock division going."

"Chris, I want to be a part of this," I said.

"Really? Why? You're not happy as an agent?"

"No, I'm sick of booking dates."

"That's great," he said. "I don't want to be stuck in an office all day. You can run this and be my man on the inside. Keep an eye on Profile."

"Fantastic. Keep me posted." I was in the record business.

Chris had me join him for the meetings that followed. Profile would provide us with space, salaries, and a marketing and recording budget for several releases a year.

I quit my job. I was looking forward to this new project, and thought that, in Williamson, I had a like-minded friend and music business collaborator. Within weeks I was on the street, broke and unemployed.

———•———

Andy split with Arne—cleaning out his desk without so much as a goodbye—and left TRA shortly after me to open his own agency, Bandwagon, run briefly out of his apartment. Somers took Megadeth, Slayer, and Testament along as clients. In 1987, he joined Ian Copeland's renowned Frontier Booking International ("FBI," home of the Police, Squeeze, and R.E.M.), and, in 1992, ICM. Six years later, he reopened Bandwagon in Los Angeles. In 2001, Somers was tapped by agent Steve Martin to open the West Coast office of The Agency Group. He continues to work with Martin to this day.

I worked with Andy on a couple things over the next few years and we talked occasionally. However, we didn't stay in touch. Over the past few decades I watched as his personal narrative evolved. In contravention of facts, Somers now never cites his time at Talent Resource Agency in his bio. According to his own lore, "he began his career at Bandwagon, the New York-based independent booking agency he founded in 1984." Somers apparently woke up one day, possessing the prescience and ability to sign Megadeth, Slayer, and others out of his one-man bedroom operation—a good year before I joined Talent Resource Agency.

———•———

When I started at Rock Hotel Records in early 1986, Profile was riding high on Run-DMC's recent release and was about to drop their groundbreaking *Raising Hell*. The company had just moved into gorgeous, newly built offices on Broadway at Astor Place. A comfortable room had been set aside for us, with desk space for three or four people.

I was still certain this was an exciting opportunity to create and grow a label that could offer an alternative talent source to the parent label. With the combination of Chris' and my background and experience in the early-stage niches of hardcore music and speed metal, I thought we were going to kill.

However, in the new setting, I was stunned to find Chris dismissing my advice … that which he used to eagerly seek. He had somehow decided he didn't need my—or any—help running the label, and went so far as to accuse me of "forcing him" to hire me. I still can't process this turn of events. When I tried to move our relationship back onto a more positive footing, he even cited his friend Gary Tovar's distaste for me as an illustration of my failings. I was seeing another side of the mercurial Williamson personality.

I now questioned his ability to fulfill his new leadership role. It was confirmed when he lamely suggested I take on the label's radio promotion duties. This would primarily involve me speaking with college students around the country. There's also the fact that I wouldn't have left TRA for a job in promotions even at a major label! I'd had a good thing going as an agent, working directly with artists, managers, and promoters, as well as liaising with record labels. I had simply tired of it. I hadn't been with Chris at Rock Hotel long enough to sharpen a pencil … and I certainly wasn't going to stay to do a job I didn't want with a guy who no longer wanted to work with me. We parted ways.

Rock Hotel Records put out a dozen or so releases of varying quality. Sales were uninspired, and Profile did not renew its arrangement with Chris. He continued to promote concerts for a while until fading from sight. He emerged briefly in 2002 with a short-lived Rock Hotel classical piano concert series. Last I heard, he still lives on his houseboat. Look him and Rock Hotel up in books and online today and you won't find many nice things said about him. Most are true. My experience, sadly, ultimately jibed with those accounts.

———•———

That spring and summer, with the sounds of Run-DMC's singles and videos, "My Adidas" and the monster hit, "Walk This Way" as a constant background reminder, I plotted my next course.

I involved myself with negotiating the Splatcats' recording deal. However, managing a garage band with no album release was not going to pay the bills; I needed money.

At the same time, I lost my room in the Soho loft. My roommate was getting married and her husband was moving in. They didn't want to adopt me. I began a classic New York City real estate-hopping journey of room rentals and sublets, including a stint with David Keeps, the editor of *Star Hits*, the US version of *Smash Hits*, a leading British music magazine.

Keith Rawls was the new NYC-based manager of Megadeth. He'd been installed by his friend, and pre-TRA business partner, Andy Somers. Rawls heard about my situation and offered me a desk and a phone in his West Village basement office. He threw me a few bucks to answer the phones, take messages, and help him out.

I wasn't thrilled to be working with Mustaine again, especially so soon after I had said goodbye to everyone at TRA. But the allure of eating overcame that distaste. And besides, I didn't harbor any illusions that I was involved in Megadeth's career. Keith and I were helping each other out. And in fact, my interaction with Mustaine was minimal. He called the office a few times and left messages, and we chatted amicably when he stopped by to visit Rawls.

I finalized the Splatcats contract with Celluloid. Their record, *Sin 73*, was released on the Celluloid imprint Moving Target. (When you turned the album upside-down, the title read "Elvis.")

During my time at Rawls' office, the annual New Music Seminar, one of the biggest music trade gatherings on the East Coast, was happening.

Megadeth was, of course, invited to attend the convention, and Rawls had name badge passes for his act. The band, regrettably, was not in town. The Splatcats, however, *were* in town to promote their new release. Guess who went to the NMS as "Megadeth"?

At the huge event, the guys from Buffalo—who generally dressed in boho '60s type rags—were instantly identified by those in the know as NOT Megadeth. Others, who lacked a visual reference, were fired up to see the hot metal group, though possibly confused by the gentle wardrobe and demeanor. The boys took it with characteristic humor, and made the best of the opportunity to promote their new album.

———————•———————

By now you may be asking, where's all the sex and drugs to go along with this rock & roll story? Well, I'm not a kiss-and-tell guy, except where specifically noted. Sure, I was in the biz ... lots of bands and folks I worked with wanted to check out strip clubs and other R-rated (and beyond) joints. Yeah, I joined them. I'm a dude. And there were debauched music industry affairs I attended whose secrets will die with me. Except for the one in which a drunk friend of the groom at a bachelor party went home to his wife with a used condom still attached to his pecker. She wasn't too happy about that. However, I don't know if that necessarily reflects the music business.

Drugs were not of much interest to me unless they affected someone I was working with, so some drug use is depicted throughout my tale. I couldn't dissuade others from abusing themselves. And, sure, I smoked pot in high school and for a few years afterwards, but it got boring. I tried cocaine in my early days in New York. Then *tried* it some more. But I'm going on the record here to say it wasn't America's "war on drugs" or Nancy Reagan's "Just Say No" '80s campaign that halted my limited recreational use. It was the death of Len Bias who, two days after being selected by the Boston Celtics as the number two overall pick in the 1986 NBA draft, died from a cardiac arrhythmia induced by a cocaine overdose. It was attributed to be related to his height. As I'm a tall guy, I never touched the drug—or any other illegal substances—again.

As long as we're talking about what's not in this memoir, you might also be wondering if my mother and father make appearances again. A little, but not so much. This isn't that kind of a story. Maybe the next one. If you are looking for a good book on dysfunctional family life, I'd recommend *Running with Scissors* by Augusten Burroughs, *The Ice Storm* by Rick Moody, and *Fun Home: A Family Tragicomic* by Alison Bechdel. You could also try *The Family* by Ed Sanders.

The Mercenary years: 1987-1988

In the first months of my involvement with the Splatcats and Celluloid, my relationship with the label's founder and president Jean Georgakarakos developed. He was a French-born Greek rogue, also known as Jean Karakos.

He'd started in the music business in France at age 20. With money he'd made selling life insurance door-to-door, he imported American record albums, produced and released avant-garde jazz records, and presented concerts. He'd developed very sophisticated taste in music.

When I met him in NYC, he was 46. Celluloid had been a critically lauded independent record label for a decade. When Celluloid enjoyed both financial *and* critical success, much of it was attributable to Karakos' collaborations with musician/producer Bill Laswell of Material. (In 1982, Laswell cowrote and produced Herbie Hancock's "Rockit," a huge hit and one of the era's most played music videos.)

Celluloid put out recordings by world music giants like Fela Kuti and Manu Dibango. Karakos was also an early promoter of hip-hop, with releases by Grandmaster D.ST and Fab 5 Freddy. Bill Laswell produced the Last Poets and the Golden Palominos for the label, as well as *World Destruction* by Time Zone, which paired Sex Pistols/Public Image Ltd. frontman John Lydon with Afrika Bambaataa.

Celluloid was located at 330 Hudson Street, in an eight-story 1910 brick warehouse that was home to manufacturing businesses and open-floored lofts. The neighborhood was known as "The Printing District" for its high concentration of commercial presses.

The sunlit Celluloid space contained a warren of private drywalled offices surrounding a big, open space, where the promotional and sales staff worked. In the back warehouse area, a couple of guys constantly received, picked, packed, and shipped records from inventory.

As I got to know Karakos a little better, I took the initiative, and proposed I start a metal label for Celluloid, since it had already diversified to rock recordings, like Richard Lloyd (Television), the Fleshtones, the Splatcats, and others.

He immediately recognized the value of such an imprint, with me at the helm, and gave his OK. The industry, including Karakos, was becoming aware that heavy metal bands of all kinds were making waves in both the independent and major label worlds.

Through the Splatcats deal, I had learned how challenging it was to get Karakos to part with money. He would eventually pay what was owed or promised, but collecting it was excruciating.

During negotiations at the Ear Inn, one of the few nearby restaurants in the Printing District (and one of the oldest bars in New York City), I saw an opening.

"Jean, what would you say to giving me a desk in the office so I can directly supervise and educate your people on this new metal genre?"

Karakos considered this and agreed. I launched my next prepared salvo, knowing how difficult it might be to get paid if we actually *did* sell any records.

"How about providing me with an advance on sales on a weekly basis? As long as I'm in the office, you could issue the check along with your regular payroll."

I suggested $200 a week. Not a great sum, but I was on my ass. If he said yes, it would be huge. Through a mouthful of quiche and salad, Karakos said: "Let's make it $400. The $200 will be an advance against record sales. For the other $200, you'll help me out with my bands, publishing, contracts, and anything else."

Karakos had recognized me as a kindred operator. I had a record label, an office, and had just hired myself a new boss.

———•———

I came up with the hard-hitting name Mercenary Records. Its tone matched that of the genre. I envisioned a logo with a fist holding a rifle in the air or a "metal" medieval knight's glove holding a mace or battle-axe. This would mirror the imagery that many bands used.

We wanted to set ourselves a cut above the rest. With the help of a talented graphic artist, we settled on a metal-gloved hand holding a chain against a shield. It resembled a family crest, and was slicker and more professionally rendered than other metal labels' logos.

My deal with Karakos included providing Celluloid with a finished master tape and album cover art, which they would then manufacture, press, and distribute under the Mercenary imprint. I would receive royalties on sales and publishing, and retain certain long-term interests in the contracts. I would have sole creative control over which albums were released and what the artwork, advertising, and promotion looked like.

Record labels normally pay artists to record, but in this case, I'd sign them with the agreement that the first recording was their responsibility. I was confident there were enough groups willing to deliver finished masters for the opportunity of a national release and payment on the back end. As the records came out, I would guide Celluloid personnel in promotional and marketing activities.

———•———

I decided to introduce Mercenary with a compilation album. This type of project—featuring unknown or lesser-known bands—was an organic and low-cost way to find and expose artists, especially in the early metal days. A label could put together a release sourced from demos.

Finding compilation producers to shepherd the talent, people who necessarily had contacts with bands to feature, helped us acquire acts that had already built up some insider cred. An added bonus was that these bands were often under the radar, still unknown to other labels.

Upon release, we could gauge how the audience was responding to the tracks, and see which, if any, were generating more interest than others. With that developing buzz—and the assumption of future sales—we would offer those artists recording deals for full-length albums.

So far, I had not been deeply involved in securing unsigned talent. Most of the bands I booked while I was an agent had already signed record deals by the time I began working with them. Now, to find some groups, my first call was to my old friend Richard Sanders, the booker for L'Amour.

Richard and I had continued to develop our professional relationship. He also managed bands, including White Lion. His know-how and drive were about to help the band achieve platinum status. I relied on his counsel and his networks; he'd also helped me find the first apartment sublet, on the upper west side, that was all mine.

"Richard, I'm starting a metal label," I said. "It's called Mercenary Records."

"That's a fantastic name, tell me more."

I explained I was looking for artists, and that I wanted to put out a compilation album featuring newer acts playing at L'Amour—under the L'Amour banner. Since it needed to be done on the cheap, I told him my plan to fill the album with demos and available tapes.

"Let me talk it over with the club owners," he said.

Within days, Richard had approval from the club. He had already come up with the name, *L'Amour Rocks*, and would be the executive producer. He enlisted metal tastemaker Chuck Kaye (the club's house DJ, known as the "Roar of L'Amour") to help select and secure the songs. (Eddie Trunk, a DJ just starting his career, provided the liner notes. His name was regrettably misspelled

"Truck" on the album sleeve. Trunk became a prominent hard rock and heavy metal radio and television personality.) We were on our way to our first release.

As the L'Amour demos and recordings came in, I was impressed enough with a few of the bands to sign them to deals right away.

———◆———

As most people know, artists are signed to labels in a variety of ways. However it happens, it's usually due to some combination of talent, fate, timing, and luck.

David Wolin, of the Splatcats, and his wife Nancy Brennan sent me a demo tape by friends of theirs from Buffalo: Goo Goo Dolls. Not coincidentally, Cal Zone had been listening to their demo and had mentioned them to me around the same time. I remember grunting when he did, thinking, "That's the stupidest band name I've heard in ages."

When Dave and Nancy gave me the tape though, I immediately gave it a listen. From the first tune, the songcraft was apparent. It seemed a natural fit as a release on Celluloid's Moving Target label, which was dedicated to rock and college-radio acts like the Splatcats. And with Cal's support, I figured I could land them a deal. If Karakos was interested, I hoped to add the group to my management roster.

"Jean, you have to hear this tape right now," I said, hardly containing my excitement.

The skeptical, heard-it-all Karakos told me to come into his office.

He listened. Halfway through, he shrugged. Someone listening nearby said: "They sound like the Replacements." Karakos turned off the tape.

"I don't hear what you hear, Dean," he said. "But I can see you're into them. Why don't you sign them to Mercenary?"

My vision for Mercenary did not include a band like this. The demo, and their early high-energy style, owed more to punk than metal. They were still evolving toward the musical sound that helped them attain commercial success.

Nevertheless, I agreed to make it an initial Mercenary release, not wanting to lose the opportunity to be involved with the group.

———●———

I also signed Primal Scream NYC, whose lineup included Keith Alexander from the thrash band Carnivore. They had recently added the "NYC" to their name when they realized there was another band called Primal Scream—in Glasgow. While these New York rockers weren't exactly tuned in to the UK indie-pop scene, to be fair, at the time no one was expecting much from Bobby Gillespie's now-influential Scottish outfit.

———●———

Mercenary's first three records were delayed, mostly owing to Celluloid's cash flow and Karakos' seat-of-the-pants business style. Karakos and his company didn't observe formal release dates or bother with detailed marketing plans. This meant that, only when a Celluloid manufacturing bill did get paid and when the album eventually arrived in the warehouse, the in-house sales staff could get to work selling it. Considering the nature of the independent record world, it was not wise for anyone under this regime—salespeople, artists, or imprint label heads—to expect a timely release. It wasn't always the best way to develop trusting relationships with the artists and managers, but most, even if disappointed, understood that "these things happen."

The Goo Goo Dolls, however, chose not to understand this concept. They even removed my name from their personal acknowledgments over the course of the album art design. Still, wanting only the best for the band and my records, I continued enthusiastically.

The Mercenary titles trickled out. It was common practice to create promotional posters. For our label launch, ours featured

L'Amour Rocks, Goo Goo Dolls, and Primal Scream NYC's *Volume One.* The headline read: "A landmine in the face of conformity," and a massive iteration of our logo was set above images of the three albums.

We also made a separate marketing poster for each LP. We proceeded to radio and retail promotional efforts. Karakos, spirited by the attention the label was receiving from his employees and other colleagues, approved hiring a dedicated Mercenary publicist. I drew my candidates from the underground metal fanzine community.

It was a thrill to see my records and posters "end-capped" at major retail outlets like Tower Records, an international music sales giant. This meant that we paid a premium to have the product displayed prominently at the end of an aisle, giving it competitive advantage.

————————●————————

Another band I signed was Meanstreak. They are likely the first all-female thrash metal group. In the male-dominated bastion of heavy metal, I got a lot of negative feedback for that move. The message was that they were a "novelty act." I just thought they were good, and deserved a wider audience.

Meanstreak's record came out to positive reviews. They were soon opening for both leading and emerging metal artists, including Anthrax, Overkill, Flotsam and Jetsam, and Motörhead, proving to many that they were not a novelty. They reflected what was happening in garages, clubs, and recording studios around the world.

I also moved into licensing albums by more commercial, "radio-friendly" bands.

Many internationally based, major label artists can't get a record released outside of their home country. With the band or their management eager to get anything put out in the United States, I could pick up major label titles for next to nothing. These albums were recorded by top producers with substantial budgets, meaning that for little advance outlay and the cost of manufacturing and promotion, we could release records that sounded as good as any stateside major label product. Groups like Canada's Kick Axe and Germany's Victory licensed us their work. We received some great radio attention for Victory's "Check's in the Mail," the lead track on their album. A few office wags dubbed it the Celluloid theme song.

Albums sold, and I earned my keep; although, with the exception of *L'Amour Rocks*, nothing really sold well. Being on premises, I knew exactly how many records we were selling. I was right there, and had my eye firmly on the inventory … and Jean's books.

———•———

In the winter, I called Andy Somers, now at Frontier Booking. I asked him to consider taking on the Goo Goo Dolls. Somers agreed to add them as the support act on a club tour for a Boston band he was working with, Gang Green.

There wouldn't be a lot of money for the group; they'd be roughing it. But it was a good opportunity for them to be seen, and sell some records in the spring.

I had recommended a Buffalo-based manager and concert promoter, Artie Kwitchoff, to road-manage the tour. Kwitchoff had impressed me with his ability to make things happen for the hometown bands he represented. I even offered him a free desk at Celluloid if he wanted to move his hustle down to New York City.

A few weeks before the Goos set off touring, bassist Rob Takac called me with concerns about Artie. I assured Rob that he remained a good choice. Bands and road managers touring in vans often develop a good relationship from the intimate traveling conditions. I presumed they would bond with Artie after time spent on the road. Rob relented and Artie went out with them.

———•———

I also still had managerial responsibilities with the Splatcats. Their album did well, receiving college airplay and wonderful press. My proximity to Karakos within the office helped ensure a second album release.

The band and I met with Jeffry Katz about producing the Splatcats' next album. Katz was one half of the Kasenetz/Katz hit-making duo known professionally as Super K Productions. The two producers literally created "bubblegum music" in the 1960s, coming up with the name while churning out hits for bands and manufactured concepts like the Kasenetz-Katz Singing Orchestral Circus, the Music Explosion, 1910 Fruitgum Company, and Ohio Express. The pair scored again in 1977, when their production of "Black Betty" by Ram Jam landed on the US top twenty and charted in other countries. The idea was met with stone-faced indifference from Karakos, so we settled for a producer from Buffalo.

The Splatcats' *Feelin' Bitchy* came out in April of 1988. The record was strong, and we were revved up for solid college radio attention. Wolin was still the leader, though the group underwent lineup changes—precipitated by a grievously stupid attempt by one of the band members at knife-juggling the week before a planned tour.

After incredible work by the promotional crew at Celluloid, *Feelin' Bitchy* reached the top ten on the *College Media Journal (CMJ)* charts. It was a tremendous accomplishment in a highly competitive arena; many major labels, with their deep-pocketed resources, vied for the same airplay and chart position.

Through my contacts, I connected the Splatcats with an agent in London to book them in Europe. Lesser-known American artists like them could achieve enough press from European publications to translate into media attention or major label offers back in the US. Additionally, overseas exposure could generate offers from European labels to license our US recordings.

Karakos arranged for a substantial amount of export inventory—the band's albums that we'd released in the States—to be available in the foreign markets where the Splatcats were performing. And, he promised to provide some financial support to defray touring expenses after we returned.

This would require me to advance the costs required to launch the tour—London hotel and food when they arrived, equipment rental, transportation for the gigs, the overseas publicist I'd hired, plus pay the European road manager a couple weeks' wages before they hit the road. I applied for an American Express card and they kindly (and shockingly) obliged.

Amex's credit policy was a complete mystery, especially to a new cardholder. The prestige business card required full payment each month. And the credit line they extended was at their whim, so you never knew how much was available, or if a charge was going to go through.

I would join the band for the flight to London, and ensure everything was in order on their arrival. I purchased our plane tickets with the Amex and crossed my fingers that I would be able to use the card in England.

A couple of days before we were leaving, I headed over to my bank to grab the few hundred bucks in my account so I could throw something to the publicist and road manager. At the vestibule ATM, I entered my PIN and waited to check my available balance. It showed I had over $30,000. I blinked to clear my eyes, a cartoon-like reaction to a ridiculous situation. Was this a test? A trick? I looked around to see if anyone was watching, considering my options. I initially cancelled the transaction. Some people might have reported the mistake right away, but my solution, at that time, in my circumstances, was to walk into the branch and fill out a withdrawal slip for $10,000. This was too good to pass up, even though I knew it was on borrowed time. And "borrowed" money.

I handed the teller the slip. She punched my details into the terminal.

Instead of my anticipated, "I'm sorry sir, you don't have enough funds in your account," she asked, "What denominations would you like?"

"Hundreds please," I calmly answered. Funds in hand, I headed out the door, waiting for security to stop and cuff me.

I cleared the exit, and with the ten grand stuffed in my pocket, giddily headed home. Well, now I didn't have to worry whether the American Express card would work. The cash would be there as a back-up. And I'd redeposit it when I got back in a few days. I assumed someone would eventually notice the error. And at worst, if I had to spend any of the cash in London, Karakos' tour-support check would cover things when I returned. I relaxed just a tiny bit.

On the Virgin Atlantic flight, Wolin and I roared as we watched the in-flight movie, *Planes, Trains and Automobiles*.

The flight attendants gave out complimentary Virgin-branded toiletry bags. They fit snugly in one's hand like a small book. I brought mine into the bathroom and wedged about 9,000 bucks into it. Landing at Gatwick, we cleared customs and headed to the Commodore Hotel near Hyde Park.

At check-in, I set my Virgin amenity kit on the counter. The Amex went through. No need to dig into the cash. I handed everyone their keys and we headed to our rooms.

As I unpacked, it dawned on me that I should secure the cash. I looked around for the pouch. Holy shit! I left it downstairs. I tore out of the room and called the elevator. The ancient lift lumbered up and jolted to a stop. I jumped in and smashed the lobby button non-stop until the doors closed. I was like a caged animal pacing the tiny space, flipping out.

Arriving at the lobby, I rushed to the check-in area. The front desk guy saw me moving towards him with a deranged expression. He looked terrified.

"I left my Virgin bag!"

"Yes, sir. It's right here." He handed it to me. People probably left stuff at the desk all day long, especially these prized freebies. His look morphed into one that said: "Why is this giant Yank so worked up about his sample-size toothpaste and moist towelette?" The cash was still there. I breathed a sigh of relief and the money never left my person again. I went to take care of business.

I paid a visit to the publicist and laid some cash on her; the road manager, too, was the recipient of some of my largesse. I secured the van and equipment for the boys. The credit card did its job. At that moment, I had the feeling that everything was going my way—I was confident that my destiny was sealed and my success ordained.

The Splatcats set off across Europe. I had meetings in the city and checked out the sights. Back in New York, I returned the remaining cash to my account. A few days later, the bank noticed their error and left me with a negative balance, without saying anything to me. For once, it didn't take a crowbar to separate Karakos from the coin, and he handed over part of the promised tour support. I was able to cover the overdraft, and no one was the wiser. Sadly, unable to pay the Amex bill, it took me years to restore my credit. As American Express has a remarkable corporate memory, I am currently not a valued member.

———•———

I continued to supervise Mercenary and help Jean with miscellaneous business, mainly acting as a buffer between him and various musicians who were seeking monies owed.

Record labels were entering a period of huge transition and growth. Compact discs were becoming widely accepted. Vinyl was fading; by 1988, CD sales surpassed those of vinyl records. Many consumers chose to replace their existing record collections with compact discs. Recording companies' back catalog sales surged as fans repurchased their favorite albums. With wholesale and retail cost of compact discs considerably higher than vinyl albums, record-label profit margins soared. The music industry was swimming in cash—collectively heading into the 1990s with unprecedented optimism.

But Karakos was slow to fully adapt. The bands and I looked forward to seeing our records on this exciting new technology, the "CD." But rather than manufacture CDs simultaneously with a new vinyl album release, he took months to get them out. Some of it was due to his inability to obtain a decent line of credit from CD manufacturers. Jean's reliance on Bill Laswell to prop up finances had also become unsustainable, since the producer had moved on to work with paying clients like Mick Jagger and Yoko Ono. Laswell even got into the metal game, producing Motörhead. Karakos found himself deeper in debt. Staff was let go, and other budget cuts were made.

Beset by financial distractions, and requiring more privacy than the office afforded, Karakos began operating out of his home much of the time. A minute's walk from Celluloid, he and his wife had a large, high-ceilinged garden apartment. Arriving for an impromptu meeting, I'd often find Karakos ensconced in his bed, situated in the middle of the flat like an Egyptian barge. He conducted business from there, in a weakened state due to his subscribing to a mish-mosh of holistic and Eastern religious practices. During his long-term ritual fasts and cleansings, he claimed that "food was bad for you." I found this a bit paradoxical as he had always enjoyed the incredible homemade pies at Ear Inn. Under his influence, and as evidenced by my slightly expanding midsection, I now embraced his devotion to dessert.

———•———

My arrangement with Celluloid called for them to pay the artist royalties directly. Most of the Mercenary bands received a little money for sales here and there. In many instances, on a historic day that Celluloid would actually send artists their royalty statements, the envelopes were missing the most important element: the check.

Somehow, even when musicians and managers went into Jean's office angry, demanding to be paid, they'd come out empty-handed, yet laughing. A pat on the back from Jean sent them on their way. He was persuasive and charming, when he wanted to be.

Thanks to the moderately successful *L'Amour Rocks* album, my pal Richard Sanders was owed a bit more than others. He was having trouble collecting. He appealed to me, and I went to bat for him.

"Jean, could you please pay Richard? He's a friend and a figure in the metal world." This was a modification of the requests I'd been making for other artists and managers.

"Jean, seriously," I said.

"Look, Dean, I'll meet with Sanders and explain that this is a challenging time. He'll understand," the rogue-in-chief said.

I called Richard, who'd always been an above-board business-man. I jokingly suggested he bring L'Amour's largest bouncer with him when he met Jean. He laughed.

It wasn't Richard's typical tactic, but he actually took my advice and showed up with a big security guy a few feet behind him. Jean ushered them both into his office. Richard winked and smiled at me on the way in. And this time, someone left with a check for payment in full.

———————•———————

I'd signed a group called Powermad from Minneapolis. Soon after-wards, major label Reprise expressed interest in them. Contracts are often sold, and Reprise contacted us directly to see if they could buy the Powermad agreement. I hoped for a nice payday for me and Karakos.

Meanwhile, the Goo Goo Dolls were in Los Angeles, with Kwitchoff, the road manager I had insisted they use. Kwitchoff had already insinuated himself into the band, and elevated himself to manager. Mercenary and I became the enemy. As a further twist of the knife, and unbeknownst to me, he arranged to have a rep-resentative from Brian Slagel's Metal Blade Records see the band perform—Kwitchoff's sister knew a Metal Blade employee who grew up in Buffalo. Metal Blade was as unlikely a home for the group as Mercenary was; nonetheless, they wanted to sign them.

Instead of either Metal Blade or Kwitchoff coming to me or Jean to talk it out and make a deal for us to release the Goo Goo Dolls from their recording agreement, Kwitchoff hired a Buffalo-based personal injury lawyer in an attempt to nullify their contract with us. He took the fanciful position that "Celluloid's contract with the band was no longer valid." When their attorney reached out to me, I still believed we were on the same team. The connec-tion to my hometown community and friends of the Splatcats was still stronger than my relationship with the ever-slippery Karakos. I explained the best way to accomplish the band's move to Metal Blade. I commiserated too candidly about Karakos's business practices. The lawyer surreptitiously taped our conversation and sent a transcript to Jean.

The rancorous situation with the Goo Goo Dolls affected my relationship with Karakos. He stopped paying me and terminated our arrangement. Karakos also sought to push me out of Powermad's Reprise deal, keeping everything for himself. My only recourse was to file multiple lawsuits against Celluloid and Karakos. Months of legal wrangling followed. Luckily, I had a good friend who was an attorney willing to take this on, as I never could have afforded to pursue it otherwise.

(The lawyer representing me was my high school friend, Casey Fundaro, who had relocated to NYC. Casey's uncle, Danny Hutton, was one of the founders of hugely popular rock hitmakers Three Dog Night. When Casey was a kid, his uncle took him along to a Three Dog Night stadium concert, where the starstruck young music fan got to meet opener Marc Bolan backstage. Bolan gifted Fundaro his tambourine. This would have been a great origin story if Casey had achieved his dream and made it as a rock musician— his burning talent imbued with transcendental powers transferred through the doomed rocker's instrument. For an attorney specializing in slip-and-falls, not so much.)

The suits were settled. I got the rights to a few records, including the Goo Goo Dolls' album and recording agreement.

Powermad did sign with Reprise. The group's time there was marked by a notable achievement—they appeared in director David Lynch's *Wild at Heart*, with Nicolas Cage and Laura Dern. Powermad shows up in a club scene, performing their own song; they then back up Cage singing an Elvis Presley number. The film won the Palme d'Or at the 1990 Cannes Film Festival.

The Goo Goo Dolls signed with Metal Blade. I elected not to fight to retain the band. I sold the group's Mercenary album to their new label in 1990 for a modest price, in a deal that also included royalties on sales of those recordings. Mercenary was no more.

———•———

As many early-stage bands do, the Goo Goo Dolls continued to "sleep on floors and play for doors"—that is, no hotels (either fancy or sleazy) and their only income a share of what people paid to get into the club.

The band soon parted with Kwitchoff and signed with Roven-Cavallo Entertainment and their associated company, Atlas/Third Rail Management, a Los Angeles firm that handled Prince and Paula Abdul. There, Pat Magnarella (Weezer, Green Day) became their manager.

Warner Bros. Records, whose distribution arm had been working with Metal Blade, took a more active involvement in the Goo Goo Dolls. The band fired their drummer along the way.

In 1996, the group filed a lawsuit against Metal Blade, claiming the contract they'd signed with the label was "grossly unfair, one-sided, and unenforceable." It was essentially the same thing they claimed with Mercenary, though with decidedly higher stakes as the Goo Goo Dolls had begun to sell records.

In settling the dispute, the band moved to Warner Bros. Everyone involved ignored my agreement covering the sale of the first Goo Goo Dolls recordings. I never saw another royalty payment. Since signing with Warner, the group has sold more than twelve million albums worldwide.

———•———

Karakos' troubles continued. The IRS padlocked Celluloid's doors for unpaid taxes. Jean was able to sell the company for a dollar; the buyer assumed its debt of over a million dollars. Karakos and his wife were thrown out of their apartment together with their belongings. He was literally on the street.

Down on his luck, but debt free, back in France, Karakos was still possessed of drive and hustle. He was inspired to launch a label focused on Brazilian music. He scraped up enough for a round-trip air ticket to South America. In Porto Seguro, he went out to a dancehall.

In the club, beautiful young dancers of all genders were shaking it up to a unique regional sound he had never heard. It melded merengue, salsa, and reggae—it was called "Lambada." He bought every Lambada record by local bands that he could get his hands on.

Returning to France, he organized a group of musicians to interpret and record the sound. He made an arrangement with CBS/Sony France for its release. In the summer of 1989, a cut culled from those sessions became the biggest single in France and went on to sell over five million copies worldwide. The release was the most successful European single in the history of CBS. The Lambada became a global phenomenon and generated income from multiple sources for Karakos.

Karakos had failed to credit the writers of the songs he'd appropriated, and ended up having to relinquish half his rights. In spite of that, he was now a rich man. In 1994, when he heard that the businessman who took on Celluloid's debt defaulted, he purchased the entire Celluloid catalog back from the bank. Never one to leave a franc on the table, legitimate or otherwise, when Karakos sold the label's catalog, he'd included several of the titles I had retained in my lawsuit, which he no longer owned. He died in 2017.

Nothing but noise: 1989-1992

I secured a new record deal for the Splatcats with a company in the Netherlands. Wolin left the group and moved to New York City. Nothing much happened with their European-only release. They broke up.

A Celluloid colleague, Geordie Gillespie, asked me to manage Konk, his post-punk dance band. I was hustling as usual and agreed. The group was formed in 1980, and while it was fading, had a good pedigree. Trumpeter Shannon Dawson had played in the band Gray with Jean-Michel Basquiat. (Shannon's niece, Rosario Dawson, would be "discovered" while sitting on her front step a few years later.) The actor Richard Edson (*Stranger Than Paradise*, *Platoon*, *Do the Right Thing*), who was also Sonic Youth's original drummer, had been in an earlier iteration of the group.

Konk's music had just been used in the film *Bright Lights, Big City* with Michael J. Fox. We negotiated a 12" single called "Konk Blast" with 4th & B'way, an Island Records imprint.

The band had an underground recording studio on the Lower East Side, on Ludlow Street between Stanton and Houston. The area was in the early stages of its transition from a traditionally immigrant and lower middle-class neighborhood to the hipper hotbed it is today. The building was adjacent to El Sombrero Mexican restaurant. The studio was *really* underground; you had to stomp on a cellar door (two rusty metal sheets covering a deep hole in the sidewalk, like a storm shelter) to gain entrance.

One day, as I was waiting at the door for a band member to let me in, ten police cars, sirens blaring, manned two to four to a car, appear from all directions converging near where I was standing. Plainclothes and uniformed cops spilled out of their vehicles. It was a drug sweep on the street dealers and buyers. A barrel-chested, badge-on-a-neck-chain, plainclothes cop ran full-throttle directly towards me. Before I could let out what surely would have been an inappropriately shrill shriek, he had me face first against some solid steel window bars.

"What are you doing here?" the cop barked.

Between trying not to evacuate my bowels, with my lips and teeth pressed into metal, I couldn't choke out a word. A local guy who I'd never seen before ran over. "He's with the group, he's with the musicians, the recording studio there," pointing to the cellar door.

After processing what this guy was saying and apparently assuaged, the cop released his grip on me and moved on, telling other officers in the area to ignore me with a dismissive wave in my direction. My liberator stood by for a few minutes, still fending off cops by saying, "He's with the band." I was shaking for at least an hour. A street guy I ain't.

Hopes that the Konk single would lead to a new album did not pan out. This post-Mercenary interval was difficult, marked by financial challenges and career concerns. But my reputation in the metal world was still secure.

By late summer of 1989, I parlayed my experience into a job at a German heavy metal label, Noise Records, which was headquartered in Berlin. As label manager, I would take over day-to-day management of US operations.

———•———

Savvy music industry veteran Bruce Kirkland—whom I'd met through a friend—hired me to work at Noise Records. Kirkland rented an entire floor in a warehouse building otherwise filled with garment sweatshops, at 5 Crosby Street, on the edge of Soho and Chinatown. In addition to living there and subletting space to Noise, Kirkland was running his own enterprise, Second Vision, a marketing firm that developed and supported campaigns for major and independent labels and musicians. He was also the de facto label head or manager for overseas businesses—like Noise—that needed someone to watch over their US operations and licensees.

The New Zealand-born Kirkland had earned a law degree in the early '70s, but was more drawn to concert promotion. He'd met Stiff Records cofounder Dave Robinson on an Australian Graham Parker tour. Stiff launched in the UK in 1976. (Its motto: "If it ain't Stiff, it ain't worth a fuck.") A fundamental part of the international new wave music movement, the label's roster included Elvis Costello, Ian Dury, Nick Lowe, and Madness. Robinson hired Kirkland to join him in London. Kirkland moved to New York City in 1980 to run Stiff's US office.

When I joined Noise, Second Vision was in demand and at the top of its game—with a client list that included Erasure, Peter Gabriel, Kraftwerk, Primal Scream, Psychedelic Furs, the Sugarcubes, Swing Out Sister, and The The. Bruce supervised the American operations of UK-based Mute Records. As the label's US conduit, he was deeply involved in growing Depeche Mode's career. The electronic group was one of the most popular synth-pop bands of the 1980s. In 1988, Depeche Mode performed a history-making concert at the Rose Bowl Stadium in Pasadena, California—selling out the 65,000-capacity venue.

A highly motivated contingent of entrepreneurial-minded people worked for Bruce. Successful and up-and-coming musicians, executives, and managers constantly streamed through. In the morning, it was common to see Bruce laboring across the floor in his bathrobe, navigating the office hallway between his apartment and his private bathroom. One might find themselves unexpectedly bumping into Nick Cave using the fax machine. The casual atmosphere belied the effective work being conducted.

———•———

Noise was founded in 1983 by Karl-Ulrich Walterbach, a self-pro-claimed anarchist. His hardline stance had softened, and he was now fond of eating at hip restaurants and wearing unconstructed sport jackets with rolled-up sleeves.

Noise's bigger acts included Helloween, Celtic Frost, Kreator, and Voivod. Other "big in Germany" bands on the label—like Running Wild, Tankard, Rage, and Grave Digger—were known only to the most ardent US metal fans. Watchtower, Mordred, and Coroner rounded out a deep catalog.

While at Noise, I learned how the professional end of the re-cord business functioned. It was fun and stimulating, marked by travel, a good salary, an expense account, and comfortable living.

But first, I had to figure out how to work with the extremely disgruntled staff I'd inherited.

———•———

Noise Records was distributed in the US by CBS. When I joined the company, Karl had fired the previous label manager. The remain-ing employees were demoralized and frustrated, as well as loyal to their former boss. They barely hid their resentment. As their new leader, I did my best to lift their spirits. It wasn't really working, so I decided to just get to it.

I reviewed our CBS product requests and uncovered nearly $100,000 in back orders of CDs and cassettes (another dwindling yet still viable format). In the open-floored office, I said aloud, "Why aren't these orders filled?"

The staffers all expressed a shared opinion that "no one was going to buy our records, so there was no reason to manufacture them."

While I was still a relative record company neophyte, I had confidence in at least one dictum: Albums definitely wouldn't sell if they weren't in stores. I instructed them, still grumbling, to fill the back orders.

I set about hiring for an empty sales and marketing position, adding Tom Derr to the organization. Tom was a focused and deliberate guy with an intimate knowledge of retail. He had five years of experience in music retail as a seller and buyer. As sales and marketing director, he would communicate with the distributor, stores, and other record sellers, ensuring they were aware of the label's product and that they knew to access our releases through CBS or other sub-distributors. When Tom sent in his resume, he was working in the mailroom at A&M Records. I saw he needed a chance to prove himself. Tom stepped into the position and was immediately in play, without any direction from me.

We received our first monthly statement and a check from CBS reflecting the back orders I'd pushed out. Karl happened to be in New York, and came by.

"Can I see the new CBS statement?" he asked warily.

I sensed he'd posed this question to my predecessor many times, only to be disappointed. I handed him both the statement and an image of the just-deposited check. He looked back and forth over the two items, confused. Then he looked at me, and tore out of the room. I thought for sure I'd blown it. I was heading to the streets again.

My phone rang. Bruce. I was asked to join him and Karl. The walk down the hall felt like my last mile. Arriving at Bruce's office, I was having trouble reading the room, though Walterbach *appeared* to be smiling.

"Dean, this is incredible! How did this happen?" Karl said. He and Bruce were beyond impressed. We decamped for a celebratory lunch, to discuss ideas, plans, and "the future."

————•————

The cash flow that month, and over the next few months, stabilized Noise's US operation. The breathing room allowed Karl and Bruce to seek a new distribution deal.

While CBS was generating new sales, their interest in Noise was waning. I had inherited too much history with CBS and Noise.

CBS had also been acquired by Sony. Noise was getting lost in the shuffle.

Karl and Bruce began conversations with RCA Records and BMG Distribution. BMG (Bertelsmann Music Group), a powerful and influential German consortium with offices throughout the world, was the parent company, or had ownership interests in, RCA, Arista, and many other record labels and publishing entities. In the US, its distribution arm handled the sales of recordings for those mainstays as well as an array of independent or associated labels like LaFace, Zoo, and Jive. Notably, RCA and BMG were the homes of Elvis Presley, respectively releasing and distributing his forty-plus studio, soundtrack, and live albums.

BMG and RCA were logical places to do business. They were already familiar with Noise's potential for identifying talent. RCA had picked up the Noise band Helloween's *Keeper of the Seven Keys: Part I*. The album was an international success, charting in Germany, Japan, the United States, and other territories.

We soon had a deal with BMG that included a bridge agreement with RCA to pay us an advance for the first option to move any of our bands to its label. Noise left CBS Distribution.

With the new BMG Distribution arrangement, and some RCA money, we were off and running. Tom and I created a presentation video introducing Noise, and took it on the road. Armed with promotional T-shirts and buttons declaring, "Noise Records: Elvis has *really* left the building," we visited all the BMG regional sales branches, as well as many record chains and independent stores around the country. We established a great working relationship with BMG Distribution.

———•———

Using my Goo Goo Dolls proceeds, and with a job in place, I leased my own apartment. It was a small loft studio on 12th Street, near the Strand Bookstore. My days of real-estate hopping were over, and I settled into living in Greenwich Village. It was my last apartment in NYC.

I adjusted to my new status, living and working downtown again. I entertained in my home. A blender filled with frozen margaritas was permanently adhered to the kitchen counter. My personal and professional lives also blended seamlessly. Tom and his wife came to my house for parties; we hung out together, going to concerts.

Bruce and I occasionally socialized outside the office. Once, he brought members of Depeche Mode over to my pad, and we watched a pay-per-view boxing match.

After quitting his band and moving to New York, David Wolin was working as a sales guy at Caroline, an independent record distributor. Caroline was flush with success, representing such labels as Sub Pop, Matador, Epitaph, Touch and Go, and its own imprint, Caroline Records. David, his wife, Nancy, and I got together to watch (and agonize over) Buffalo Bills games.

———•———

I attended and presented at a bunch of conventions, including those sponsored by BMG, National Association of Recording Merchandisers (NARM), National Association of Independent Record Distributors (NAIRD), and Concrete Marketing (a specialty heavy metal promotion company).

In this era, I reaped some music-biz perks: In Los Angeles, I stayed at the Sunset Marquis (known for its celebrity clientele), rented sports cars, and ate at hip spots like Sushi Nozawa and the Pacific Dining Car, wolfing down a strip steak at 2 in the morning. I even had an occasional breakfast meeting at the Beverly Hills Hotel. Back in NYC, Gallaghers Steakhouse became a favorite.

RCA optioned Noise albums by Swiss metal band Celtic Frost and (Helloween member) Kai Hansen's Gamma Ray. With a major label push behind them, we were optimistic. But, as can happen in this business, by the time the releases were ready, the team who had championed the records at RCA was gone—moved on or fired.

The new RCA president, Joe Galante, had overseen RCA's Nashville operations. Commercial country music was booming.

Under this new leadership, not unexpectedly, our inconsequential metal albums floundered.

Yet, as sales were strong with our releases through BMG Distribution, the staff grew. I hired a fresh set of people who were ready to work with me, instead of against me. One by one, I let the old employees go. Some were probably just as glad. One of the reasons might have been that Tom and I tortured them with *Tales from the Brothers Gibb*, a forty-eight-song Bee Gees box set, in constant rotation on the office CD player.

————————•————————

A phone call came in from the manager of a Boston-based metal band I was somewhat familiar with. "Sure, I'll take that," I said, not catching his name.

He started his pitch. I was having trouble understanding him. I'd been to Boston, and even had friends from there, but I'd never heard an accent this pronounced. It must have been an obscure dialect, made stronger through the generations. I wasn't sure I could work with somebody like this, let alone get past an introductory phone call. But, you never know where the next big thing is going to come from. Maybe he had speech impediment? I'd managed with plenty of guys with heavy Northern English and Scottish accents by now. I tried to be polite and soldiered on.

"Yes, please send me the band's latest material. Give me your number—what's your name again?" I ask.

"Mock," he says.

"Mock? That's an unusual name," I reply nonjudgmentally, more as a leading question.

"Mock," he says, more slowly, as though he were talking to a child.

"Right. I got it." I spell it out for him: "M.O.C.K. And your phone number?"

"MOCK! MOCK! Not MOCK!" he says, his voice rising.

In our now-escalating Abbott and Costello routine, I say again, "Mock, yes, I got it. What's your number?"

He shouts, "MOCK! MOCK! MOCK!" and slams down the phone.

I have to hand it to him: He still sent the demo. Though we didn't sign the group. Why didn't he just say, "No, M.A.R.K."? Good old Mock.

At least that's how I prefer to remember it. Here's what really happened:

I *think* they had initially approached Karl and he asked me to deal with them, which is probably why I picked up the call. I knew the band had released an album with Rock Hotel, and I wasn't that interested in working with them.

The conversation as related above did happen, and the demo arrived. We considered it seriously, but ultimately decided against signing the act, and let them know. That's how business works, guys.

However, less than a week later, I received a 9 x 12 manila envelope with a Boston postmark. It was soiled, beat up, and didn't seem to contain anything—maybe the contents had fallen out. It only took me another second to realize what was going on, and I didn't need to open it. Someone associated with the band had jerked off into the envelope and sent it to me. Like I said, good old Mock.

———•———

Walterbach was itching for a hit for Noise. He signed London, a Los Angeles heavy metal outfit, bucking current trends and best advice from cognoscenti and tastemakers.

London formed in 1978 in Hollywood. The group was known more for its constantly shifting lineup than its intermittent album releases. Lead singer Nadir D'Priest had been recruited in 1984, and he drove the band's longevity, whether that was something to brag about or not.

Playing with the band became a rite of passage, or "rock & roll high school," for Los Angeles metal musicians. After having cycled through the group, it was as though you'd touched a talisman. Former members of London founded, or joined, Guns N' Roses, Cinderella, Mötley Crüe, and W.A.S.P.

In 1988, London had appeared, somewhat unflatteringly, in Penelope Spheeris' film *The Decline of Western Civilization II: The Metal Years*.

While recording their release for Noise, Walterbach continued to hear from the naysayers. London's reputation was tarnished in the US. It's not *just* that they weren't "hot"—many (both within the industry and their own fans) believed they were past their prime.

Walterbach invested a lot of money in recording the new album, *Playa Del Rock*, which was produced by Richard Podolor (Alice Cooper, Three Dog Night). In late-1990, as it was being readied for its US release, and perhaps fearing more negative reactions, the band and Walterbach decided to change the name of the group—*in America only*. The record would be a "London" release in Europe and was listed as being by an artist named "D'Priest" in the US.

This was shaping up to be an epic disaster. Still, we forged ahead.

An expensive-looking promotional video was commissioned to support the first single, the charmingly titled "Ride You Through the Night." You read that right.

The four-minute video opens, sepia-toned, with a stampede of horses. A mystery man rides through the desert on horseback, shown only from the waist down.

An Old-Western motif is introduced, including cow skulls and a few band members in Western garb. One of the long-haired musicians, in contemporary attire, pulls a couple of video vixens in period dress out of a Conestoga wagon.

The video transitions through another horse stampede to a modern-day scene, and segues to full color. We see several big Harley-riding guys rolling across the desert in the sunshine. Remember, the song title references riding "through the night."

We are treated to the sight of the group set up in the middle of the desert, performing the song. Interspersed are cuts of a bare-chested D'Priest writhing on the ground in the throes of sexual passion and additional scantily clad models.

Both the album and the video were ready for release and promotion. This style of music video was appropriate to the era and typical of the genre, and got airplay on MTV's specialty metal program, *Headbangers Ball* (where they censored the title to "Ride Through the Night"), and other video outlets. The video also garnered positive response from retail record sellers when it was screened at music industry conventions. Still, the album bombed.

The group broke up in 1991. D'Priest periodically tried to revive the act. As London, the *Playa Del Rock* lineup gave a reunion show at the Roxy Theatre in Los Angeles in 2010. In 2012, he led a new lineup through some dates in Europe. A *London Live!* album was released in 2013. The band released a new studio album in 2018. D'Priest still hasn't given up on London.

———————•———————

Dennis Dennehy came in as publicity director. He was just out of college, and he'd aced his interview, displaying a sense of humor and an acute knowledge of contemporary new music. He wasn't part of the heavy metal community. I was hoping to help diversify the label, and had a hunch he could grow into the recently vacated position.

We sent out a press release regarding the hiring. A columnist from music trade journal *Billboard* called me. They asked if there was anything I wanted to add to the announcement about Dennis.

"I'm pleased to have found someone who can spell properly," I deadpanned.

That's all *Billboard* printed.

———————•———————

My mother and stepfather (husband number two out of four) visited me from Buffalo. Their dining tastes ran to the provincial and price was absolutely an object. Their favorable restaurant reviews could usually be distilled to, "It was great. The portions were huge."

I took them to La Mela, a Little Italy spot known for its family-style servings of pasta-and-cheese laden specialties. Located on a densely packed block of Mulberry Street, upon entering, you couldn't help but notice framed celebrity photos lining every inch of available wall space—attesting that the food befitted the rich and famous.

As our bacchanal was nearing its conclusion, Jackie Mason and an entourage entered the place. The Borscht Belt comic was enjoying a career resurgence; he'd recently starred in several successful Broadway productions, and also been cast in some bigger-than-usual film and television roles. The host ran up to Mason and his party. His training definitely included fawning over stars of any level.

"We'll take care of you, Mr. Mason," he said, surveying the room and zeroing in on our table. "Come back in five." The Mason group moved from the doorway to the street.

As soon as they were clear, the host, while sprinting toward the back of the restaurant, pointed at us and barked orders to the waitstaff. Someone brought our check and the busboy started clearing our dishes. We literally couldn't object since we were still chewing.

The host, a bit flushed, returned with something in his hand and thanked us for "agreeing" to move along. As we shuffled out, he matter of factly plucked a photo off the wall near the table we'd recently quit. He inserted a jauntily signed picture of Jackie Mason there. He might as well have buffed the frame with his cuff.

Despite the bum's rush, my mother and her husband were happy. They had a celebrity sighting *and* leftovers.

———————•———————

Once again, musical tastes were changing. Newer metal subgenres like thrash and speed had marginalized a lot of the European power metal groups, an area in which Noise specialized. "Hair metal" (Poison, Cinderella, Ratt, Warrant, Extreme) was also in its last days. Even with the thrash and speed bands, the wheat was being separated from the chaff.

In May of 1991, *Billboard* contacted me for a quote on the perceived decline of heavy metal. I put on a positive face. "'The decline in product sales, ticket sales, metal-oriented publications, and airplay is not reality,' says Dean Brownrout, GM, Noise Records. 'Due to the evolving definition of 'metal,' what constitutes a 'metal' recording, concert, or publication has become blurred, leading to media and public perceptions of decline of metal sub-markets. Also, any perceived decline may be attributable to some of those in the industry who have failed to change their development focus along with the rest of the evolving market.'" Blah blah.

Metal itself wasn't dead. But the '90s had ushered in new sounds. The business had moved on—"alternative" was the new-new thing, soon to become an overused buzzword. I was asked to try and bring in some alternative acts.

I signed New York progressive rockers Naked Sun, and Chicago-based Rights of the Accused, a hardcore band that was transitioning to a more tuneful rock sound. Neither release did much to revive Noise's fortunes.

———•———

BMG Distribution held an annual corporate convention for the entire company encompassing several days of workshops, motivational get-togethers, and presentations. It was attended by most every label distributed by BMG in North America.

One full day of the convention was devoted to each of the larger labels, like RCA and Arista. The companies, led by their top executives, took their time presenting their upcoming slate of releases. Clive Davis was there, among other high-profile music vets.

For the many independent labels that BMG distributed, a day was also set aside, during which they'd each get fifteen minutes to make their pitch. In 1991, Noise was invited to participate in the event, that year taking place in Toronto.

I would attend, and planned my segment carefully. You could do anything with those fifteen minutes; talk, play music, show videos, etc. I decided to give a short speech and then invite Naked Sun to perform a song live. We were about to release their first album.

I called band member Max Vanderwolf and laid it out. "This will be in front of hundreds, if not thousands, of people," I said. The band had only played for smaller club audiences thus far in its young career. I wanted to be sure they'd understand the pressures. "All of whom we want to be out there selling your record …"

"Yes, absolutely. I get it. We're excited. This is a great opportunity," Max assured me.

For an unknown band's release, Noise could generally count on an organic initial order of 10-15,000 units. That was a good starting point, and enough to ensure "coverage" in the stores—i.e., product on the shelves—to support the label's promotional efforts. It also meant the public could find one or two CDs in each record store. With Naked Sun being featured at the BMG convention, we hoped to generate enough interest to ship more.

On the day of, Naked Sun set up their gear in advance. The plan was for them to quietly assume their positions on stage while I was talking, and begin playing as soon as I was done. Our slot approached. Pete Jones, the affable president of BMG Distribution (who had a remarkable gift for remembering people's names) was introducing each label. He announced Noise and I bounded onstage. Hundreds of BMG employees and other record label contemporaries seated in the large ballroom stared.

I gave my prepared five-minute spiel, thanking the BMG salespeople, and mentioning a few recent and upcoming release highlights. The band silently readied themselves behind me.

Devoting a few words regarding what they were about to see, I wound things up with a rousing, "And now, would you please welcome, Noise recording artist … Naked Sun!"

A respectable round of corporate applause followed. I stepped off the stage, and the group was revealed in the rising lights. Rather than an immediate burst of crowd-pleasing music, only silence rang out. The band, backs to the audience, frantically pushed buttons on their amps and fiddled with their instruments. Something was terribly wrong.

At the back of the room, I had a horrible feeling in the pit of my stomach. More silence. It was probably one of the longest minutes of my life.

Vanderwolf, the lead singer, turned to face the audience. As he did, what had looked from behind like really big epaulets on his shoulders were revealed to be garishly made-up plastic doll heads, simply part of his stage attire.

Laughter, some nervous and some outright, arose from the audience. It was accompanied by more deafening silence from the band. Vanderwolf attempted to fill the void with a joke or two. Finally, in a gigantic anticlimax, they launched into their song. It was delivered solidly, to polite applause.

Following the Naked Sun "showcase," the BMG salespeople returned to their hometowns. Orders for the album dripped in; rather than the 15,000-plus we had prepared for, only 1,000 copies shipped. Most were returned, unsold.

The music industry soon took another major shift. Seattle grunge bands, the majority associated with the independent Sub Pop label, were making inroads, but in the fall of 1991 Pearl Jam's *Ten* and Nirvana's *Nevermind* bookended the Naked Sun release. The incredible success of those two recordings sent me and everyone spinning. The next sea change had arrived.

———•———

One evening, I headed uptown to grab a barstool at Arriba Arriba—still on my go-to list. It was well past midnight by the time I returned home to 12th Street.

The block I lived on, between Broadway and University, was a dense mix of loft apartments and professional offices. A large portion of the street was taken up by an NYPD building, home to some police units like the Manhattan Robbery Squad. The residents in this generally quiet section were upwardly mobile New York strivers: Wall Street traders, early-career doctors, entertainment industry types, working actors. A young Jon Stewart lived in my building for a spell.

A year earlier, a pool hall called Le Q had opened on the ground floor of the building adjacent to my apartment. It was frequented mainly by NYU students, and had a predominantly Asian clientele. Patrons rarely hung out on the street for too long, and as far as I knew, there was never any trouble because of the billiards parlor.

When I got home that night, though, a police officer was standing at the entrance to my building. He asked to see my ID before allowing me to enter. In front of the poolroom, yellow police tape blocked sidewalk access. "There was an incident next door," was all he offered when I asked him what was up.

The morning news revealed all: three young men wearing black ski masks had walked into the hall, approached a table, and fired automatic weapons, specifically targeting an individual or individuals. The other sixty or seventy customers screamed and took cover. One person was killed, and three others shot in the hail of bullets.

The gunmen backed out of the building and sped away in a waiting car. A few police detectives happened to be walking nearby, noticed the commotion, and saw the men take off. The officers gave chase on foot, catching up to the vehicle at 9th Street and Fifth Avenue. The suspects were apprehended.

The "pool hall rampage" made national news and landed on the front page of my hometown paper, *The Buffalo News*. By the time my mother frantically called to express concern and worry, the yellow tape was gone and I had largely forgotten about the occurrence. Tragic as it was, such was the blasé nature of the entrenched New Yorker I had become.

———◆———

In early 1992, Noise's relations with both RCA and BMG began to turn. RCA no longer saw us as a viable farm-team talent source and signaled that it would not renew our agreement; BMG Distribution also wasn't happy with our latest sales numbers. How could they do this to us, when we were coming up with such clever promotional items as the one for our band Coroner? In our boneheaded enthusiasm, we thought it was a real giggle to distribute a Coroner-branded "scalpel" (actually a working X-Acto knife) to support sales of the group's latest release.

Billboard caught wind of our predicament, and called to inquire if we'd lost our deals and were closing as a result. The reporter asked, "Why didn't RCA renew your contract?"

I flippantly said, alluding to the current president of RCA and his Nashville roots, "Well, I guess they're just a little bit country, and we're just a little bit rock & roll."

The reporter laughed. He got the joke … I thought. When would I learn that humor and *Billboard* don't go together?

An hour later, I get a call from an ancient-sounding attorney at RCA.

"Excuse me, Mr. Brownrout, we just heard from a reporter at *Billboard*," began the man drily. "He said you told him the reason RCA didn't renew our arrangement with Noise is because RCA is too much of a country label?"

That thudding sound was my head banging on the desk.

He continued, "Because you know, there were several reasons we elected not to renew the agreement …"

I cut him off. "It was a joke! Donny and Marie. The song from the '70s!" I said. He was befuddled.

I wouldn't have been surprised if he'd replied, "We don't do jokes around here, Mr. Brownrout."

———•———

BMG did not renew our distribution deal either. Karl and Bruce tried to find us a new distributor. While they looked, and with no great prospects, Noise was in a holding pattern. The writing was on the wall. I began laying off staff and cutting expenses. Dennis Dennehy took a job at Geffen Records. I gave him an exceptional reference and was sorry to see him go, but it was the smart thing to do. Over a period of twenty years, Dennehy worked his way up to executive vice president and head of publicity at Interscope. He had huge roles in the careers of Beck, Eminem, and Lady Gaga. As a publicist he still personally represents Eminem. I knew that kid was going somewhere.

Karl found an arrangement to keep his product distributed in the US, but it wasn't enough to warrant a stateside operation. Bruce and Karl kept me in place as long as they could, but by summer, the New York office of Noise closed. I remained in touch with Karl.

Tom Derr joined RCA's marketing department before becoming vice president of marketing and artist development at Universal Records. At the majors, he worked with the Bee Gees, Robert Plant, and ZZ Top. He was involved in the success of the Dave Matthews Band.

Noise had been around for years before I joined it, and remained in play for years after I was gone, though Karl's fortunes waxed and waned. He sold Noise in 2001. A history of the company, *Damn the Machine: The Story of Noise Records*, by David E. Gehlke was published in 2017.

Bruce Kirkland is still active in the music and entertainment industry. In the mid-'90s he was named executive vice president of Capitol/EMI and was then appointed president/CEO of EMI-Capitol Entertainment Properties, a newly formed strategic marketing and brand management division. He also remembers that time as a fertile one for those who came through the Second Vision and Noise offices.

In *Damn the Machine*, Kirkland is quoted as saying, "We were all entrepreneurs … My philosophy was about being a self-starter … everyone is doing six jobs. You learn more … the entirety of the business and how it all connects and works together."

While that period at Noise was not hugely prosperous, it was a time of pronounced professional growth for me. But nothing prepared me for what was coming down the road.

———•———

Whenever I'm asked which artist I'm most proud to have some connection to, however fleeting, I answer Jeffrey Lee Pierce.

I met Pierce in 1982 when we brought his band, the Gun Club, to the Continental in Buffalo. We booked them again later that year. On one occasion I helped the group cross the border into Canada and accompanied them for a show in Toronto. On another, I assisted them through a few Northeast dates. The Gun Club's lineup on that run included Jim Duckworth (Tav Falco's Panther Burns) on guitar, Dee Pop (Bush Tetras) on drums, and Patricia Morrison (the Bags) on bass. (As I became fast friends with the group, Pierce nicknamed me "Sex Bomb." He and the band called me that all week. Later on, I heard that Patricia had joined Goth band Sisters of Mercy; to get into one of their New York City shows, I sent my business card with "Sex Bomb" written across it to her dressing room, and did in fact receive speedy backstage access.) I had the privilege of working with Pierce again as an agent at TRA. He was touring to support his 1985 solo album, *Wildweed*.

Pierce was the former head of the Blondie fan club in Los Angeles. He'd bounced between a few minor groups there before forming the Gun Club and releasing the 1981 album *Fire of Love*. It's a remarkable debut, especially considering it cost $2,500 and took forty-eight hours to record. Pierce used his fan club connection to entice Blondie cofounder Chris Stein to produce their next release and put it out through his Animal imprint with Chrysalis.

The Gun Club's swampy amalgam of punk, Robert Johnson-influenced blues, and roots, and its impact on music and musicians at the time of its release and well after, has been well-articulated by professional reviewers. (The album is included in the book *1001 Albums You Must Hear Before You Die*.) And *Fire of Love* sounds as exciting to me now as it did back then.

Pierce's onstage persona was mesmerizing. His preternatural vocals filled the room as he ecstatically channeled Jim Morrison and Howlin' Wolf. The deeply troubled Pierce was an alcoholic, addicted to heroin and pills—it's often the first thing that's said about him. I have no interest in playing into the mythology that surrounds him. I can only agree with the universal sentiment that his self-destruction and death in 1996 at age 37 was a sad and terrible loss.

In my early travels with him, he was a mumbling, babbling mess, incoherently chattering to everyone and no one in particular from his perch in the back of the van. Later in NYC, when I was an agent, we found time to hang out socially during the tour supporting *Wildweed*. Walking around the city with Pierce, his girlfriend, and bandmates, he was thoughtful and clear-headed. We were mostly sightseeing, rather than partaking in unhealthy pursuits. The circumstances of the *Wildweed* shows the agency booked for him—underfunded, not enough venues, spotty performances from Pierce—caused the tour to devolve into a brawl. Their road manager walked off the tour in Milwaukee. So much for the version of Pierce I saw in New York.

If he had only recorded *Fire of Love* and disappeared, it would have been enough to cement his legacy. Despite his well-documented and all-too-real human deficiencies, I always saw something special in Pierce. He was literate. A great lyricist. Audacious. He left a discography that testifies to his unique talent.

———•———

Soon after Noise's shuttering, I got together for drinks with my friend David Wolin.

Since arriving in New York, Wolin had been doing good work at Caroline, where he was now its distributed labels manager. In essence, he was the liaison between the company and all its distributed labels. But he had ambitions beyond drumming and sales.

Wolin had a gritty rock musician vibe—a full set of tattoos and, depending on his mood, either shoulder-length hair or a completely shaved head. This visage was in exact contrast to the conservative-but-hip, all-black New York City armor I had developed since abandoning my earlier, preppy appearance.

To look at us, you'd think he was the up-all-night, single rocker and I was the quiet stay-at-home type. But the opposite was true. I reveled in the bachelor life, drinking and carousing till all hours. Wolin was married to his long-time girlfriend and expecting his second child. A late night was a rarity for this musician-turned-salesman-and-dad.

Over drinks, the conversation moved to what we both might do next.

"You know," he said. "*We* could start a record label."

"We?" I thought. Then I considered the easy connection I had with this smart, hilarious, hard-working rock & roller, and thought this could be good for both of us.

"Yes, let's do it," I said. It felt right.

All we had was a simple idea: Put out music we like.

For the previous ten years, I'd been primarily involved in heavy metal. I had grown exhausted by the music and its aesthetic, with its many, many umlauts, its old English typography and satanic imagery. Not to mention the volume.

I wanted to get back to releasing music by artists that I actually listened to "after work"—artists who were influenced by the musicians I loved from the early '60s and '70s—particularly the "Bs": Beatles, Beach Boys, Byrds, Big Star, and Burt Bacharach.

Wolin's tastes were broader. He had an encyclopedic musical knowledge. His preferences ran more to the rockers. He was a drummer after all. This would be a good *contrapunto* to my leanings.

I'd be the "the Beatles guy." He'd be the "the Stones guy."

We settled on the name Big Deal. We came up with the name independently, then were reminded that it was the name of the record label in the 1978 film *Sgt. Pepper's Lonely Hearts Club Band*, the jukebox musical atrocity based on Beatles songs, featuring Peter Frampton and the Bee Gees.

David and I approached Steve Sinclair, the owner of Mechanic Records; he'd formerly been an A&R manager at Combat Records. Mechanic had some modest successes with the groups Dream Theater and Trixter through MCA. Sinclair was diversifying his label and adding new imprints. We saw an opportunity to provide him with a stream of "alternative" talent. To prove it, we gave him a batch of demos and shared our label concept. Steve offered us a deal immediately. He agreed to manufacture, market, and distribute Big Deal, including modest advances to sign and record our artists. One of our first signings was the New Hope, PA band Brother Eye, managed by Steve Garvey of the Buzzcocks. Their first album for us was produced by Mercury Rev's Dave Fridmann, whose projects with bands like the Flaming Lips and countless others ultimately earned him a Grammy, and distinction from *MOJO* magazine as "the Phil Spector of the alt-rock era."

———————•———————

A friend from the business, Scott Givens, who worked at Roadrunner Records, gave people nicknames that stuck. The husky and affable Givens always had a smile on his face and a Pabst Blue Ribbon in his hand. And he really was great at the name game; just ask his friends "Beertruck" and "Psycho." So far, I had escaped any Givens-given moniker.

One night, though, I stopped by a music industry event at Roseland Ballroom. I happened to be accompanied by two attractive females (a friend, and someone she'd invited to tag along). I spotted Scott in the crowd and we went over to say hello. He jumped back a little, taking in the three of us.

"Whoa," he said. With a big grin and his eyes lit up, as if he'd received a message from on high, he pronounced, "I've got it. Your nickname is 'Big Daddy.'" Thirty years later, there are still people who only know me by that name.

A new era begins: 1993-1995

After delivering a few releases to Sinclair, and fulfilling our immediate obligations, David and I quickly realized it was the wrong fit. This guy was only in the "Steve Sinclair" business. David turned around and got us a pressing and distribution deal with Caroline Distribution. Caroline would advance us the cost of manufacturing our CDs and recoup those costs from our sales.

With essentially no money, our early signings would have to rely on the clever strategies I had practiced at Mercenary. (Not the bad tricks I learned from Karakos.)

We sought artists who had self-recorded, unreleased albums in the can. We would guarantee them a certain level of advertising and marketing support to promote their release. We also guaranteed small advances for future recordings if we elected to continue working with them. With Caroline as the distributor, the artist could be reasonably assured that their CDs would at least be found in stores, so most of them readily agreed to our offer.

I bought a Macintosh Color Classic computer (sporting 4MB of RAM and a 40MB hard drive) and a stuttering dial-up modem. I ran the label's day-to-day operations out of my 450-square-foot Greenwich Village apartment.

Wolin worked out of the Caroline office, using his influence to ensure the sales staff prioritized our product. David's wife, Nancy, a talented graphic artist, was our "art department." She designed many of our CD booklets and all of Big Deal's advertising and promotional materials.

Our closest consultant was Charlie Pye, a bespectacled accountant with an ample midsection and a hearty laugh. Pye advised several other independent record labels; he and I had crossed paths professionally. In addition to mutually respecting each other's business sense, I appreciated his providing accounting services *pro bono*—though he said he'd be looking forward to a "reward" down the line.

——————•——————

An East Village dive bar, the Coyote Ugly Saloon—in its pre-movie-infamy days—became my favorite hangout. When it opened in '93, it was just a local shot-and-a-beer joint, not the crazy, franchised, reality TV, mega-enterprise it is today.

My drinking buddy, Scott Givens, turned me on to the place. Walking into the Coyote Ugly with him for the first time it reminded me of places back in Buffalo.

I stepped up to the bar. I was greeted by the owner, a short, tough, dirty-mouthed character named Lil Lovell.

"Whattya want?" she said.

"Tequila and orange juice," I said, calling for my "signature drink."

"What kind of a fag drink is that?" she shouted above the music.

At once shocked and laughing at the top of my lungs, I settled in … for the next eight years.

——————•——————

Back when I was working at Noise, and with more disposable income than I had previously enjoyed, I'd started indulging in some personal collecting as a hobby. Informed by my interest in nostalgia and pop culture, I liked twentieth century toys and objects, including lunch boxes, cereal boxes (yes, it's a thing), space toys, PEZ dispensers, and older film and television tie-in items. (My collecting tastes have since become more sophisticated.) Along with many other treasure hunters, I haunted NYC flea markets and collectible and antique shops. I would rent a car and head to regional toy shows, also hitting stores or conventions in other cities when there on business or holiday.

Like many collectors, my purchasing and hoarding translated into becoming a dealer, as my collection grew or I'd come across bargains which didn't necessarily fit my collecting interests. So, in the early days of Big Deal, trading in these items turned into my side hustle. It wasn't particularly lucrative, but at times it was the only cash I had coming in. And it fed my collecting affliction.

This was all pre-eBay and the boom of online sales. I was selling through mail order, placing ads in magazines like *Toy Shop,* and to other dealers and collectors.

Beginning in the 1970s, and still going strong through the '80s and '90s, on the weekends, the area around West 25th Street and Sixth Avenue was filled with vendors selling collectibles, fine antiques, junk, and other objects and ephemera out of parking lots and garages. It was the beginning of Chelsea becoming the world-renowned, eclectic arts destination that it is today. Andy Warhol famously built a good portion of his collections (cookie jars, vintage watches, etc.) scouring the fleas for bargains.

On weekend mornings, often before the sun rose (and sometimes straight from a bar after a long night), I'd head to the outdoor markets as the dealers pulled out their new goods. That's when the real deals happen; before the brunch-going retail customers and looky-loos showed up.

Collectors—whether their fervor is for dolls, records, or clown paintings—will go to extreme lengths to find their grail. I would frequently see the powerful and wealthy Seymour Stein, president of Sire Records, combing the tables in those same early hours for antiques and *objets.* The man signed Madonna, Talking Heads, and the Pretenders; apparently, he also had an eye for the finer things of a material nature. He sold off his various collections over the years via auction houses like Sotheby's.

By the early '90s, I was making enough to rent a small, bright, turnkey room in a multi-floor antique and collectible co-op called the Chelsea Antique Center on West 25th. I saw the appeal of having a spot to securely store my merchandise, versus the ungodly hours and manual labor of hauling stuff, and setting up and breaking down at the flea market every weekend.

The co-op was one of several Chelsea buildings which had been converted to indoor markets with regular retail hours. My space was like a small shop (about 8 x 10 feet). The twelve-story bazaar housed dealers selling higher-end objects—from antique jewelry to vintage jukeboxes.

I kept somewhat reasonable hours, generally three or four days a week, a few hours a day. And when I wasn't on site, my phone number clearly printed on the shop's large front window allowed me to field calls from people who'd seen a covetable *Starsky & Hutch* or *Charlie's Angels* item there, wanting a price. I could easily get over to the building to open the door and make the sale. Still, Big Deal took priority.

Collecting is a great leveler; these worlds are very small, and become even smaller based on one's interests. While I only knew about Warhol by legend, I did have a couple of brushes with celebrity—those who could afford to indulge these pursuits either financially or with their time. Actor/director Penny Marshall came to me looking for Pillsbury Doughboy-related items. And actor Cliff Gorman visited, engaging me in a lengthy conversation regarding my specialty in this period. Marisa Tomei, more in the brunch-bunch category, flashed me her adorable grin as she breezed through with a gal pal.

Putting in a few hours at the shop one day, a phalanx of burly, black-clad security types materialized on our floor. They assessed the threat level that I and other nearby vendors presented. My neighbors included a secondhand Barbie shop, a cross-dressing clothing and costume jewelry dealer, and a couple of elderly antique watch guys. The leader of the detail radioed the "all clear." Then, the biggest pop star in the world, Michael Jackson, wearing a black silk mask (he was always either anticipating or creating trends), strolled into my stall. I said, "Hi." He nodded, and wordlessly took several minutes studying nearly every item in the room; the silence was unbearable. "Please let me know if I can be of assistance," I said helpfully. He nodded again, continued scanning, then turned and walked out. His security personnel surrounded him as they exfiltrated en masse down the stairs.

———————•———————

The music industry continued to grow. Overseas entertainment retailers like HMV and Virgin Megastore set up shop in the United States and expanded their businesses around the globe. Sales of compact discs continued ever upward, each year surpassing previous year's sales. Independent labels and record stores thrived.

———————•———————

A moderately successful compilation of power pop tunes was among Big Deal's first titles. While browsing a Lower East Side magazine shop, See Hear, I came across a fanzine called *Yellow Pills*. Seeing the zine brought back the music of 20/20, a Los Angeles power pop/new wave band I'd loved as a teenager. They had a song on their 1979 debut called "Yellow Pills." I wondered if the zine could be connected to that song and era. If so, this was exciting. That would mean there might be someone out there who shared my interest in such arcane artists and musical moments.

I never liked the name "power pop," but it's a convenient and easily understood way to describe this genre: melodic, hook-filled, and heartfelt. There was a brief Los Angeles-driven power pop scene in the late '70s/early '80s influenced by that same music. That's what I wanted for Big Deal.

Yellow Pills, the self-released, Xeroxed zine, was devoted to all things power pop—past and present. Its existence, and the devotion demonstrated by its editor and founder, Jordan Oakes, showed that there was a vital audience of musicians and fans who matched my ardor for this sound. It was a lot harder to find one's community online in those days. There were no viable search engines yet, and CompuServe and AOL "bulletin boards" were rudimentary at best.

I got in touch with the St. Louis-based Oakes, and after quickly establishing we were, indeed, of like mind musically, suggested we put together a compilation for Big Deal, centered on his fanzine.

What Jordan delivered was beyond anything I could possibly have envisioned. He had relationships or access to almost every power pop band.

Big Deal's *Yellow Pills: The Best of American Pop!* was a mixture of legacy artists, alongside a new generation of musicians devoted to songs with catchy melodies and hooks. Acts on that CD included Dwight Twilley, Shoes, Tommy Keene, the Cowsills, Adam Schmitt, and even 20/20. The bands provided us with high-quality, previously unreleased material, much of which had already been paid for by their major labels.

We ended up putting out a total of four *Yellow Pills* compilations. Other well-known talents who contributed to the series included Redd Kross, Matthew Sweet, Material Issue, and the Posies.

———•———

I loved to spend time in Miami in the winter. By the '80s, once-thriving Ocean Drive hotels and residences on South Beach had fallen into disrepair. Flophouses and drug dealers abounded. It was still a beautiful place to visit, and the architecture striking. I was more comfortable staying in Bal Harbour at the (now-tragically demolished) Morris Lapidus-designed Sheraton. When the hotel was known as the Americana, its Carnival Supper Club was a hangout for Frank Sinatra and his Rat Pack pals. John F. Kennedy visited there the last week of his life.

The early '90s saw the area experiencing a comeback. I still appreciated the historic connection to a fading Miami lifestyle in evidence at my preferred hotel and at delis like Wolfie's on South

Beach, and sister outpost Wolfie Cohen's Rascal House up the road in Sunny Isles Beach.

I would try to visit every year, no matter what my financial circumstance. With the false start of Big Deal over at Mechanic Records (*we'd never see a dime from that arrangement*), I hadn't earned any significant income since Noise. My savings were depleted. I had a lot of nerve vacationing. Regardless, I charged a flight, hotel, and car on my nearly maxed-out credit card. I couldn't believe they even gave me the car. I had about 100 bucks on me, not enough to do much of anything. Still. Miami.

On my first full day, I headed to the scenic Gulfstream Park horse track. I figured I could spend the day watching the races, placing a few $2 bets, and while away the hours like the Florida old-timers do. I'm not a big recreational gambler, but I know my way around a track. Givens and I used to go to Belmont Park back in New York once in a while.

I grabbed a *Daily Racing Form*, settled into a sun-drenched seat, and scoured the prospects. One of the races featured four experienced jockeys whose names I was familiar with from Belmont. They were pitted against local jockeys who didn't seem to have much of a track record. The entire field of horses they were running against also seemed outclassed. I seized my opportunity, thinking "the fix was in"—a typical gambler's hunch. Picking the four New York horses, I boxed a superfecta. That means I selected what I thought would be the first four horses to finish *in any order*. Superfectas are not an easy hit, but many tracks offer low minimum wagers that let bettors gamble on a big payout without too much risk. The $1 combination cost $24, allowing for 24 possible outcomes. Should this strategy fail, I'd be out 25 percent of my Miami fund. Still, being so poorly financed on this trip, I didn't see much of a further downside.

The wager paid off. The four horses I'd picked came in … 1-2-3-4! I went to the betting window and collected about $650 on my $24 gamble. Like any good Miamian who just nailed the *super* at

Gulfstream, that evening I ate at Joe's Stone Crab, a classic Miami establishment at the foot of South Beach—opened in 1913. I enthusiastically scarfed down a Beefeater martini (rocks, olive), an order of jumbo crabs, hashed brown potatoes, creamed spinach, and a slice of Key lime pie.

———•———

One *Yellow Pills* contributor, Enuff Z'Nuff, had a fully recorded, unreleased album they had used to get a deal with a major label, ATCO. The label dropped the group, even though they'd landed on the charts with the songs, "New Thing" and "Fly High Michelle."

The band owed more to the Beatles and Cheap Trick than the late 1980s "hair metal" acts they were aligned with. Enuff Z'Nuff agreed to have us put out this earlier work.

As we readied the CD art, lightning struck. Shock-jock Howard Stern, a long-time Enuff Z'Nuff fan and hugely popular at the time, consented to write the liner notes for this release. We knew we had our first big winner.

The album, called *1985*, immediately sold 25,000 copies. That's like a gold record for an independent label our size. Especially with almost zero overhead because you're operating out of your living room.

Promoting the CD, Stern invited the group to appear on his nationally broadcast morning radio show. The band asked me to join them. In Stern's studio waiting room, as the guys prepared for their segment, bandmember Chip Z'Nuff said to me, "We'll try and get you on with Howard."

During the interview, Howard and Chip mostly talked about one of Chip's testicles. When the conversation turned to the album, Chip did start to talk about me, trying to get Howard to put me on the air. When Chip said my name, he pronounced it "Brown-root." Groan. Howard didn't ask me to join them, preferring to continue with the testicular issues.

Bands. Rule #1: Learn how to pronounce the name of executives you're working with.

After the broadcast, I stopped by the Caroline offices for a victory lap, proud that the band had been on the show. One of their marketing people, Dalton Ross, greeted me, "Hey 'Brown-rooooot,' what's up?!" He called me that for years. Despite his not-that-funny repetition of this mispronunciation, Ross was actually a witty guy. He became executive editor at large for *Entertainment Weekly*, and host of *EW Live* on SiriusXM.

———————•———————

Big Deal licensed several of our early albums to Karl Walterbach for European release, as he was diversifying Noise. Caroline also gave us advances against future sales, since our first albums were doing so well. With strong cash flow, we were able to offer artists modest recording budgets.

———————•———————

David and I felt strongly about each of our CDs. Not that anything could be considered a "hit." And there did turn out to be few releases made more interesting by their failure.

Here's an abbreviated list:

We added singer-songwriter Boo Trundle to our label. True story: We literally had to wait for the stars to realign while negotiating with her. She refused to sign while Mercury was in retrograde. That should have been a clue.

Idle, an alternative rock band, never met its potential. One of their guitarists ended up working for us in marketing and sales. He was great at the job, but still couldn't help his own group.

Hip, indie-rockers Milf choked under pressure. They played their best shows to almost-empty houses and imploded at more consequential performances, like showcases for key press and major label A&R people.

There was a movement afoot to bring academic poetry "recitals" to more popular audiences, via readings and "slams" in more casual settings, like music venues. On *Relationships from Hell,* our only spoken-word CD, the brash music journalist and biographer, Nick Tosches, and critically acclaimed poet Regie Cabico (now referred to as "the Lady Gaga of spoken word") were among those who presented their work. I don't think a single copy sold.

———•———

The one that got away was a group called Pinwheel (sometimes spelled "Pinnwheel"). We pursued them with a multi-pronged approach: pizza and beer at my apartment, a lot of compliments, and good old-fashioned human interaction.

Pinwheel's main members, Adam Schlesinger and Chris Collingwood, were talented musicians and great songwriters. They were stuck in a bad production contract, which prohibited them from releasing their music. There was nothing any of us could do, so we left it open and moved on.

We weren't the only ones who became aware of their song-writing abilities. Later, their legal issues solved, Schlesinger and Collingwood formed Fountains of Wayne. They signed to Atlantic Records. The producers of the Tom Hanks film *That Thing You Do!* also approached Schlesinger and asked him to pen the movie's title track. Fortunes can change fast in the entertainment business. Only a few years after sitting in my living room eating pizza, bemoaning their contractual problems, Adam and Chris had an album out on a major label and Schlesinger was nominated for an Academy Award for Best Original Song for his contribution to the film soundtrack.

Schlesinger's career ended up spanning over two more decades; he won many awards and achieved EGOT-nominated (Emmy, Grammy, Oscar, and Tony) status.

———•———

Big Deal's power pop-oriented releases received favorable reviews in almost every alternative press outlet in the United States. *Billboard* did a cover story featuring us and the genre's resurgence. Finally, a favorable mention in the key industry trade!

I had sniffed out another trend. Other bands and labels mining the power pop sound began springing up around the country. A scene developed, especially on the West Coast, where, notably, power pop had commercially emerged years earlier. It remained a niche market, but we grew our catalog and our roster. By the end of 1995 we had put out nearly thirty CDs.

The big deal: 1996

Hot on the heels of the *Billboard* feature, the label was the subject of a flattering story in *New York Press*, a free alternative weekly that attempted to compete with the *Village Voice*. Its circulation hovered near 100,000. The article by Dawn Eden, who was also responsible for the *Billboard* piece, perfectly encapsulated David's and my background and philosophy. Eden praised our "major-label quality artwork and sound, plus a certain je-ne-sais-Big-fucking-Deal-quois that's lacking from most majors."

After a few years of running Big Deal, and riding this tailwind of good press, David and I realized that if we were to grow (and pay off my Coyote Ugly tab), we needed capital.

In the current environment, labels like Sup Pop (Nirvana, Soundgarden, Mudhoney) and Matador (Liz Phair, Teenage Fanclub, Pavement) pointed the way for us, demonstrating what could be achieved from humble independent beginnings. These higher-profile indies were making deals with the major labels—Matador had entered into a partnership with Atlantic Records in 1993, and in 1996, Capitol Records was rumored to be purchasing a 49 percent ownership in the label (which they officially announced in June). And, in 1994, Sub Pop formed a joint venture with Warner Music Group. The $20 million deal gave Warner a 49 percent stake in the company. Other indie labels and artists were attracting offers of enormous sums from the majors, too. Epitaph Records (NOFX,

Rancid, the Offspring) was reported to have turned down a partial purchase offer of $50 million.

To help us seek a strategic partner, we were referred to an attorney named Barry Platnick. With his winning smile, Gordon Gekko hair, and custom-tailored suits, Platnick exuded success. His practice focused on all areas of the music business, and he had a deep network of industry contacts. We paid him a $10,000 retainer and began making the rounds of the major labels in New York. Undercapitalized, as always, it was a big gamble for us.

———————•———————

I flew to Los Angeles for a few meetings. With my interest in film noir, hard-boiled crime fiction, and insider histories, I viewed the city through a lens of characters and locations from movies like *Chinatown* and James Ellroy novels.

It was my first time staying at the Argyle on Sunset Boulevard. Formerly the St. James's Club, and now known as the Sunset Tower, the hotel is one of the finest examples of Art Deco architecture in Los Angeles. Many celebrities lived there in earlier times, including Jean Harlow and Howard Hughes. An oft-repeated myth persists that, when he was in residence, iconic American actor John Wayne kept a cow on his balcony so he could have fresh milk every day.

While on the West Coast, I met with Priority Records—home of some of the most important hip-hop and rap artists—as well as now-historic imprints. Apparently considering diversifying, one of its A&R staff expressed interest in Big Deal and reached out. It was a good meeting. I was struck by the label's fortress-like security, starting at reception. I visited my old colleague Bruce Kirkland, at this point a top executive at Capitol Records. I felt an involuntary thrill to be in the landmark building and the US home of the Beatles.

Early on, Big Deal had established a relationship with Cherry Lane Music Publishing, giving our artists an option to sign with an active and respected publishing house. If they accepted the deal, the publisher would give the acts a small advance. Other services would include collecting their airplay royalties, aggressively promoting their compositions with other performers, securing film and television placement, and even marketing their songs with sheet music. Many of our artists chose to work with them.

The publishing firm was founded in 1960 by music producer and manager Milt Okun, out of an apartment above the Cherry Lane Theatre in Greenwich Village. From there, Okun, a former junior high school music teacher, launched the careers of Peter, Paul and Mary, went on to produce John Denver's best-known tunes, and ended up representing the publishing of Elvis Presley and Dreamworks among the 150,000 songs in the Cherry Lane catalog. (BMG purchased Cherry Lane in 2010 for an estimated $100 million.)

By this time, Okun was the publishing house's elder statesman, living in Beverly Hills while his nephew handled the day-to-day operations back in New York. Upon hearing that I would be heading to Los Angeles, the folks at Cherry Lane arranged for me to visit Okun as a courtesy call. I thought it would be an honor to meet such a respected and seminal figure in music history.

At the appointed time, I pulled up to Okun's gated mansion, rang the intercom and announced myself. Like in the movies, the gates silently swung open, and I drove my rental car up the driveway. So this is how the other half lives. Swell.

His wife greeted me warmly at the door, ushering me into his home office adorned with the requisite wall-to-wall gold and platinum records and memorabilia. The unassuming gentleman joined me there.

Genial small talk ensued. Okun asks me, "Where are you staying?"

"I'm at the Argyle," and then, just trying to keep the conversation moving, I say, "I heard John Wayne used to keep a cow—"

Okun stops me with a wave of his wrist and a world-weary shake of his head. Duh. This guy probably rubbed elbows with

Wayne and here I am relaying stupid tourist stories. Regardless of my naiveté, he spent an hour with me, graciously asking about my label and my relationship with Cherry Lane. He shared some actual, true Hollywood stories. I came away from that encounter with a deeper understanding of where a long and successful career in show business can land you.

———•———

After a couple months of marching through corporate offices, no major-label deal was forthcoming. As partner prospects grew dim, Platnick guardedly brought up an investment possibility for us at a downtown startup; he'd had a casual chat with its management.

While checking out the trades, I opened up *Billboard* and saw the mustachioed picture of an old acquaintance, Tom McPartland. He was formerly a senior legal affairs executive with BMG, distributor of good old Noise.

The story said that McPartland was forming a new venture, Paradigm Music Entertainment (PME). The endeavor would include a record label, Paradigm Records, and other music business investments. They obviously had a few exciting things going on.

The article also revealed its board of directors. The impressive group included Frank Barsalona, Louis Falcigno, and Robert Meyrowitz. Barsalona, a top agent, was the chairman of Premier Talent. In the 1960s and '70s, Premier essentially created the rock concert market as it exists in the US. Among his many clients were the Who, Led Zeppelin, Jimi Hendrix, the Yardbirds, and U2. (He was the first agent to be inducted into the Rock & Roll Hall of Fame in 2005.) Falcigno was a pioneer in closed-circuit television boxing events. Prior to home pay-per-view, Falcigno established a network of satellite uplinks, dishes, and projectors to broadcast major fights to thousands of restaurants, bars, and auditoriums around the country. Each site sold tickets, of which Falcigno earned a significant share. High-profile bouts that he broadcast included Ali vs. Frazier, Leonard vs. Duran, Leonard vs. Hagler, and Tyson vs.

Spinks. Meyrowitz, a salesman-turned-entrepreneur, created the *King Biscuit Flower Hour*. The innovative syndicated FM-radio show debuted in 1973, and featured recorded concerts and interviews with rock's biggest stars. The lineup looked great on paper.

I called Platnick to see if he might be able to get us a meeting.

You already guessed it, right? Paradigm was the "downtown startup" Platnick had been in contact with. He was pleased to hear that I had a history with McPartland. I called Wolin to share the news.

He said, "You're not going to believe this! I just had a meeting with McPartland and a guy named Bob Buziak regarding Caroline business." Now it was my turn to be excited.

"Hey! I know Bob, too," I said.

Buziak had been the president of RCA Records, prior to "Country" Joe Galante. He had brought Noise into the fold. Buziak was now advising Paradigm. There were too many happy coincidences. We needed to talk to these guys about our record company. Platnick lobbied for us, and got a meeting. As soon as we could, we sent a business plan, CDs, and a press package to the new PME offices on Irving Place.

Wolin and I met with McPartland and Buziak over the summer and fall of '96. I was reminded how humorous and intelligent McPartland was. We had that ideal "vibe" that you want when you start something like this. We were all sold.

PME was backed by a group of private investors as well as DH Blair & Co., a Wall Street brokerage that put in $3 million to get things going. Blair focused on investing in very sexy, very speculative companies. They saw the entertainment industry as a way to enhance their portfolio in that direction. McPartland referred to an "internet strategy." There was already talk of an IPO (an initial public offering of stock in the company).

Feeling the pressure of our growing pains, Big Deal's finances were stretched thin. A lot of artists were heading back into the studio to work on their second albums. They required recording budgets and advances.

In addition, we had a licensing deal for the first album by the Los Angeles pop band the Wondermints. They'd already been noticed in Japan, but hadn't had a US album. Still, there was a lot of buzz about the group. This was in large part owing to a Mr. Brian Wilson.

After hearing these amazing musicians—who clearly idolized Wilson's Beach Boys—Wilson said, "If I'd had the Wondermints back in 1967, I would have taken *Smile* out on the road." He was referring to his mythic unfinished album, around which swirled numerous stories, theories, and hopes. If this wasn't fodder for a promotional soundbite, nothing was. (Stanton Swihart of AllMusic.com called the Wondermints' eponymous debut "one of the finest rock albums to see release in the entire decade." Later, the Wondermints ended up touring and recording as Wilson's backup band.)

We were also falling behind on covering our debt to Caroline. They were reluctant to extend us additional credit to manufacture our releases. Rather than alarming PME, our potential new partner, with our financial unsteadiness, we wanted to appear as though everything was business as usual.

We couldn't afford not to spend that money—but it was money we didn't have. A generous family friend came through with a loan. We moved forward with our scheduled productions, fulfilled our commitment to the Wondermints, and saved face with our potential investor—confidently coming into our next PME meeting with a stack of new Big Deal CDs in hand.

Back at the negotiating table, we got down to specifics. PME offered us some cash to pay our overhead and move the office out of my apartment. Our conviction that we could help them step things up on the label side was bolstered by having sighted a couple of their Paradigm Records employees playing solitaire on their computers.

We assuredly countered with the following: We would sell them Big Deal. We would also create a new division called Paradigm Associated Labels (PAL). We would run Big Deal and Paradigm Records under the PAL umbrella.

They agreed, also giving us a mandate to acquire or create other labels. We would, however, have to find a new lawyer. At some stage, Platnick switched teams and became PME's counsel. This is strangely common in the music world.

We sold Big Deal for stock in the new PME venture and took employment contracts that included the perks: corner offices, bonuses, and expense accounts. We were given 100,000 shares, and told that *if* the company went public, the stock would likely be worth about $5 a share, or $500,000.

Wolin and I gave 10,000 shares to our accountant Charlie Pye, who still hadn't taken a dime from us; we were grateful for his assistance, including closing this deal. David and I split the remaining 90,000 shares down the middle.

Something McPartland said during negotiations stuck with me: "Even if Paradigm Music Entertainment doesn't make money after the IPO, we could [all at a minimum] look forward to a great quality of life for the next five years." That sounded OK.

At home I readied and motivated myself by reading Barney Hoskyns' brilliant history of the Los Angeles music business, *Waiting for the Sun*.

In November of 1996, we started work under the auspices of our new banner: Paradigm Associated Labels. The deal closed officially on February 14, 1997—Valentine's Day. By that time, we were all feeling the love.

An even bigger deal: 1997

We moved into our offices one floor below PME HQ, on beautiful Irving Place. With our new budget, we hired about a dozen people and readied PAL's first releases.

Paradigm Records already had a distribution deal with Alternative Distribution Alliance (ADA), owned by Warner Music Group. We decided we would utilize that distribution system for all our labels. We let Big Deal's distribution arrangement with Caroline lapse.

At the same time, our new parent company purchased online music news and information websites SonicNet and Addicted to Noise as part of its internet approach, bringing the idea of going public closer. This was before a dot-com in the mix spelled money in the bank—as a matter of fact, hardly anyone knew what a "dot-com" did, much less how they earned money.

Addicted to Noise was founded in 1994 by former *Rolling Stone* associate editor and senior writer Michael Goldberg. It was the first internet magazine to include audio samples alongside album reviews.

SonicNet, launched in late 1994 as an online bulletin board (or BBS) by Nicholas Butterworth and Tim Nye, mostly provided content about music, including album reviews, and chats with rock bands and hip-hop acts. It drew most of its earnings from advertising and through a revenue-sharing arrangement with online music retailer CDNow.

The New York Times, covering the acquisitions, ran a story with the headline "Company Buys Web Site for Music News" (February 27, 1997). That's how much in its infancy this *World Wide Web* thing was. Besides terminology like World Wide Web entering the lexicon, in these early days "internet" was capitalized, "website" consisted of two words, and "online" was hyphenated.

The article discussed "the latest merger between the traditional and on-line music worlds," highlighting the two purchases that "will give Paradigm Music Entertainment one of the biggest progressive-music sites on the Internet, with a total of about 500,000 visits a month."

McPartland is quoted as saying, "the deal exemplifies how some music companies are looking to the Internet as the logical place to find new customers when the industry has been slumping."

The Times found a second, agreeing, opinion, also quoting Colby Hall, executive producer of *Spin* On-Line. "'I think, long term, it is a smart strategy,' said Hall." Big Deal was mentioned at the end of the article, as another of PME's recent acquisitions.

When I asked McPartland exactly how SonicNet and Addicted to Noise would turn a profit, he launched into a soliloquy that included phrases like "it's all about the eyeballs," "mind share," "monetizing the content," and "vertical portal"—which didn't *exactly* answer my question.

I respected McPartland a lot and I'm not a Luddite. I was excited about the promise the internet and our companies held. We had thrown our lot in with the man. But at that moment, his "new-internet-speak" made my eyes go blanker than Little Orphan Annie's. My mind drifted to the comfort of my first belt of tequila later that evening.

———•———

We tried to bring a few other labels into the Paradigm Associated Labels fold but those we approached were mostly palpably disinterested. They were either happy where they were and/or didn't share our enthusiasm for the opportunities presented by PAL. We managed a few logo and imprint deals with producers and talent sources.

Paradigm Records was staffed up prior to our arrival. We immediately dispatched the clock-burning solitaire players we'd spotted. The one inherited employee we retained was Stacy Meyrowitz. Yes, Stacy was board member Bob Meyrowitz's daughter; she'd been brought in as an A&R person. It would be disingenuous to say politics didn't play a role in our decision to keep her on. But Stacy did exhibit a genuine fire for the artists she both signed and hoped to sign. And she was plugged into a musical community that was outside our arena. She was particularly keen on an artist named Jono Manson, a fixture at Nightingale Bar on Second Avenue and 13th Street in NYC. Jono was responsible for leading a scene that spawned Blues Traveler, Spin Doctors, and Joan Osborne. We let her run with her picks.

As a component of our agreement, PME handed us a label called Archive Recordings. Through Bob Meyrowitz, we had access to a library of over two decades of *King Biscuit Flower Hour* recordings that included Bruce Springsteen, Lynyrd Skynyrd, Pink Floyd, Steve Miller, and countless others. It seemed like an amazing cache of material, and PME hoped to put out forty Archive CDs a year comprising the *Biscuit* tapes.

Archive Recordings was a one-man operation run by a replaceable PME man; it required little oversight on our part. And in reality, negotiating for these live recordings was complicated, involving a battalion of artists, managers, record labels, and attorneys—each of whom could immediately put the kibosh on any proposal.

This combination of *laissez-faire* leadership and convoluted access to the material meant that, instead of amazing vintage live albums by David Bowie, the Who, and Tom Petty, Archive released recordings by Nils Lofgren, Humble Pie, Canned Heat, and Deep Purple. Recognized names for sure, but destined to become instant "catalog," discoverable by only the most devoted fans in some dusty record-store bin. To iterate: If you didn't dig too deep, Archive looked good on paper—and that was most important to McPartland and the PME executives as they geared up for the IPO.

———————•———————

The stock offering remained a dream—its announcement was pushed back, first to spring, then early summer, then … later.

We grew concerned when Wolin happened across a magazine article that mentioned government inquiries surrounding employees of DH Blair & Co.

Paradigm Music Entertainment had also bitten off more than it could chew. Between financing SonicNet and PAL, upper management salaries, and overhead for running everything, its money began to dry up. What to do? Put pressure on the "kids."

We were instructed to start generating more income. It was much sooner than our business plan called for. But they said jump, and we did, accelerating our release schedule.

Selling the physical product of music traditionally entailed a bit of the old flimflam. It's one of the reasons the industry was populated with so many colorful characters—salesmen, gamblers, con men, criminals, entrepreneurs, and, of course, music lovers.

It worked like this: When new releases were solicited to retail by a record distributor, they were presented to a network of chains, e.g., Musicland, Coconuts, Strawberries, Peaches. They were also offered to a collection of regional "one-stops." A one-stop is a middleman who sold directly to independent and family-owned record shops ("mom-and-pops"). Major record distributors didn't sell directly to these smaller stores since they often only brought in a few items at a time or ordered a single piece to fill a special request.

The record label got paid on shipped goods, usually within thirty to ninety days. So, if stores and sub-distributors ordered a lot of CDs in a title's initial run—when optimism was high for its sales potential—the label would see increased cash flow reflected quickly in the monthly payments from the distributor.

If a recording was met with ongoing customer demand, i.e., continued to sell well, then monies consistently flowed into the label. The rub was that major retailers and the larger one-stops were allowed to return a certain percentage of unsold goods.

When retailers refreshed their in-store inventory through the distributor, they'd return older items that were no longer selling. The CDs, previously marked as "sold," were then deducted from the label's monthly statement. Ideally, you were shipping more albums than were being returned.

To increase cash flow, a label could push out certain releases. This was only sustainable if most of a label's catalog was selling on a perennial basis, or until the label had a hit or hits to offset the many returned, unsold titles. You couldn't continue to just "ship big" without an occasional hot record. Like a game of musical chairs, the record label could find itself without a chair. But as a short-term strategy, it was a useful way to get through lean times.

As we hustled to help bring in cash, private investors also provided PME with additional funding. Eventually Blair settled its government problems-du-jour and gave PME the money it needed to keep the lights on. Going public, and staying in business, could still be a reality.

———•———

I remained committed to Big Deal. While there were still no hits, we were making a name for ourselves and starting to have some fun. Big Deal released CDs by Splitsville, which included members of former Elektra Records band, the Greenberry Woods. We licensed Shonen Knife's *Brand New Knife* from MCA in Japan. Another Big Deal signing, Florida's Barely Pink, was featured in a Burdines department store TV ad with model Rebecca Romijn. We enlisted Badfinger guitarist Joey Molland to produce Connecticut group Hannah Cranna's second Big Deal CD. I'd picked a demo tape out of a pile and discovered singer-songwriter Michael Shelley, who would become a friend, collaborator, and noted WFMU DJ over the years. Los Angeles-based Cockeyed Ghost appeared on the cover of *LA Weekly*. And when we put out North Carolina's Gladhands' *La Di Da*, it was recommended in a prestigious *Billboard* magazine "Spotlight" pick, saying, "Literally every moment on this 12-track album is hook-filled, memorable, and potentially explosive ... A record whose wonders never cease."

Big Deal was even "going Hollywood." Movies and television shows utilized our music. Significantly, at the request of Mike Myers, the Wondermints contributed the title track to the first *Austin Powers* movie.

In Los Angeles, several Big Deal artists performed at the famed Troubadour during the annual Poptopia Festival in 1997. The multi-venue event was founded and had launched a year earlier; it drew bands and fans from all over the world, and was covered by the *Los Angeles Times* and other press and media.

I developed a relationship with world-renowned Creation Records. The English label was home to Oasis. Through a licensing deal, Big Deal released an album in the United States by BMX Bandits. David and I met its fabled and eccentric producer, Kim Fowley (Alice Cooper, Kiss, Runaways).

David created a dance label, Mutant Sound System, that had some success with the jungle and drum-and-bass subgenres, and artists including LTJ Bukem and the *Promised Land* series.

Meanwhile, our imprint, Paradigm Records, secured an album by former Guns N' Roses guitarist Gilby Clarke, and licensed recordings by Irish chart-toppers the Saw Doctors. The band's albums were among our best-sellers. A popular touring act, they sold out venues like New York's 1,200-capacity Irving Plaza.

We now had reason to be excited about Paradigm's upcoming CD *Little Big Man* by singer-songwriter Jono Manson. Manson contributed songs to, and was appearing in, *The Postman*, a new film directed by and starring Kevin Costner. It was scheduled for a Christmas 1997 rollout, and we anticipated capitalizing on Manson's participation in the $80 million vehicle. Warner Bros. was pinning holiday hopes on the film, and so were we.

The Postman is set in the post-apocalyptic near future of 2013. A nomadic drifter comes upon a USPS uniform and a bag of mail. Deciding to deliver it, he inspires hope for a "Restored United States of America."

The film completely bombed. It swept the Razzie Awards, taking home the Golden Raspberry Award statuette for "Worst Picture," "Worst Actor," "Worst Director," "Worst Screenplay," and, regrettably, "Worst Original Song," naming Manson among five other songwriters. It even won awards we had never heard of, such as the Stinkers Bad Movie Awards for "Worst Picture," and the Yoga Awards in Spain for "Worst Foreign Director." (The Razzies revisited the film in 2000, nominating it for "Worst Film of the Decade." *Showgirls* snagged the top prize.) Easing off a tad on the film tie-in, we continued to promote Manson's album with gusto.

The multi-talented Oklahoma-born, New York City-based singer/songwriter Bruce Henderson made an auspicious solo album debut, *The Wheels Roll,* in 1997, which we released on Paradigm Records. His band included G.E. Smith of the Saturday Night Live Band and Andy York, in-demand guitarist from John Mellencamp's group. Henderson had already been in an act signed to A&M Records, and published a non-fiction book, *Waiting,* about his experiences as a restaurant server—kind of a precursor to Anthony Bourdain's *Kitchen Confidential.*

As a side note, Henderson's album came to us through a production arrangement we had with John DeNicola. DeNicola was an unpretentious producer and songwriter whose modesty belied the fact that he had an Academy Award and Golden Globe on his mantle for penning one of the most-played songs in motion picture history—"Time of My Life" from *Dirty Dancing.*

Bruce's album picked up airplay on college stations and also landed on Alt-Country and Americana radio charts. I traveled to Nashville when he performed at the famed Bluebird Café. We got word that David Letterman liked *The Wheels Roll,* and wanted to have Bruce on *The Late Show* as a musical guest. This was characteristic of the powerful late-night host, who, if a band or record caught his ear, would give them a break. Sadly, Bruce was diagnosed with cancer and the momentum was lost as he healed. Henderson did go on *Letterman* a couple of years later to support his next CD, but by that time it would be the label's health that helped derail his opportunity.

———————•———————

While all this was going on, the East Coast's answer to Silicon Valley, "Silicon Alley" had begun to take shape. Overnight, money was pouring into startup businesses. New York was exploding. Defunct garment sweatshops near the Flatiron Building on 23rd Street were transformed into slick loft-style offices. New restaurants and bars popped up to accommodate power lunches and power cocktails. With the pending offering, we were right in the middle of it. We were on track to be one of the first NYC "new economy" companies to go public.

Paradigm Music Entertainment's forty-page, legally registered prospectus (or "red herring" to Wall Streeters) had been printed, and Paradigm Associated Labels and Big Deal were represented as key elements. We were in the big time.

In the fall of 1997, PME entered the IPO "quiet period"—the government-mandated interval limiting what information a corporation and related parties may release before a stock is sold to the public. It was also a *de facto* countdown to our possible payday.

After the hustle of the past twenty years or so, I was looking forward to putting a few bucks in my pocket. We had no financial expectations beyond going public and reaping our $5 a share offering price. I envisioned paying off my debts and having some breathing room. I figured I'd probably net around $225,000 when I sold my 45,000 shares.

It didn't go as smoothly as all that. The combination of the times, the technology, and the personalities had situated PME ideally to parlay SonicNet into a new deal worth millions for the parent company and its management.

———•———

A week before the PME IPO was scheduled, McPartland flew to Denver at the invitation of Tele-Communications Inc. (TCI) and Liberty Media executives.

TCI was the top cable television provider in the United States. Its holdings included TCI Music, which encompassed a few music-related media properties. One in particular, a cable operation called The Box, had business possibilities with SonicNet, they said.

The Box was a pay-for-play music video television channel that operated as an alternative to MTV, airing mostly rap and R&B videos by request. Finding synergy between SonicNet's online presence and The Box made sense.

However, when McPartland arrived in Denver, TCI offered him a job running TCI Music. McPartland laughed and said, "I can't do that, we're coming out with an IPO next week."

He added almost jokingly, "The only way I could do it is if you bought our company."

So they did. TCI agreed to purchase PME in a stock swap worth $30 million. The IPO was scrapped.

TCI Music's stock had been trading on the NASDAQ at around $8 a share. My payday was *still* seemingly assured. And at $8 a share, I might reap $360,000 on the open market. That would be a considerable premium over my initial expectations. And now we had a new, well-capitalized corporate parent to help us grow the label group. What could go wrong?

First off, according to TCI's policy, we had to take drug tests. I didn't care, but Wolin raised a huge stink. You'd think he worked for the American Civil Liberties Union the way he carried on. (Not to slag on the ACLU. My future mother-in-law was the executive director of the Arizona ACLU. But no more on that later.) He was my business partner, so I supported his right to rant. And rant he did, generally angering anyone who got in his way.

His threats to quit resulted in raises for both of us and the promise of executive stock options. Still, he ranted. Eventually, after considering the greater ramifications, Wolin filled his cup. Everyone at PAL passed; SonicNet had a few casualties. We were conflicted—happy to pass the test but also a little embarrassed. A record label with no drug users? We felt like a bunch of squares.

Next, we were told the stock swap would not be a one-for-one trade. Our shares would be diluted, valued at a lower rate than originally discussed. Supposedly, we'd have fewer shares in a more valuable company.

And now, because of certain government regulations, Wolin and I were not allowed to sell our shares until the fall of 1998. Fine, I had a salary. I had an expense account, and some newly promised stock options. It would all work out.

From glam to glum: 1998

W e got back to running our record labels. We were releasing solid CDs. Bands were touring. It was great to have the resources to give the artists backing and promotion. In the early days of Big Deal we'd been happy if we could buy an ad or print a poster once in a while. Now, we could afford to throw a record release party. We created full marketing campaigns that included promotional items, independent record pluggers and publicists, postcards, and even ads in major magazines.

——•——

For anyone coming of age in the 1970s, the Columbia House brand of Columbia Records' mail order music club was an initiation rite. They essentially created the music subscription model, in the 1950s as the Columbia Record Club, offering stacks of albums and cassettes for nearly no cost ("13 records or tapes for a dollar" and later, "8 CDs for a penny" and other variations on the concept). By the 1960s, Columbia House, having long since expanded to selling other top tier label releases, accounted for 10 percent of all recorded music retail sales. To participate, one simply agreed to buy a few more records at their regular price over a specific period. Its advertisements contained an easy-to-fill-out clip-and-mail coupon, displaying lists of current chart-topping records.

The ads were ubiquitous, appearing in comic books, magazines, television, and Sunday newspaper inserts. Its target audience of cash-strapped adolescents jumped at the opportunity to grow their record collections in one shot—often surreptitiously. For many young music buyers, it was their first chance to establish (or ruin) their credit with an adult company. As a pre-teen, I signed up, and each month would scour the catalog, learning about new or historically important artists from the photos and descriptions within.

Columbia House was viewed as a scourge by many parents who thought it was a scam, or realized too late what their kids had gotten themselves into. After the initial mother lode, if you didn't pay attention and order music you wanted, the "featured" albums of the month started automatically arriving, enormously marked-up, of course. Oh, and bills, too. If you failed to meet your purchase obligation, the collection notices followed you for years.

It also allowed buyers to purchase music in formats that record retailers had long abandoned, selling reel-to-reel and 8-track tapes until 1984 and 1988 respectively. By 1994, competitors like BMG Music Club had expanded the market to account for 15 percent of all recorded music sales. Columbia House's revenue in 1996 was $1.4 billion.

Paradigm Associated Labels joined the club. We made an agreement with Columbia House to carry our recordings. Seeing our CDs featured in its monthly catalog was a reminder of how far we'd come as a label—and how far I'd come in the music business.

It was impossible for me to be unmoved about this milestone. Instead of filling out a coupon to order my twelve "free" albums, here I was signing a different kind of contract. And Columbia House would now be obligated to pay us, rather than the other way around! I only hoped they didn't have too detailed a membership database. I think I still owed them $9.98 for the Eagles' *Their Greatest Hits (1971-1975)*.

———•———

One of my proudest achievements was connecting with illustrator Jack Davis. Growing up, I loved his work in *Mad* magazine, and his numerous movie posters, magazine covers, etc.—they'd epitomized the style of the era. I thought the look would be perfect for our compilation, *What the World Needs Now: Big Deal Recording Artists Perform the Songs of Burt Bacharach.*

It was. Davis's artwork for the CD depicted a swinging '60s Manhattan cocktail party. The drawing—excerpted on the cover, and reproduced fully on the inside of the booklet—hilariously caricatured many Big Deal musicians. Wolin and I, tuxedo-clad, were at the center of the proceedings.

———•———

Big Deal had a five-band label showcase at Poptopia, in Los Angeles, on February 6, 1998. Before heading to the venue, the Martini Lounge on Melrose, I learned that Beach Boy Carl Wilson had died earlier that day. I was emceeing the show, and I had intended on dedicating the evening to him from the stage. In the tumult of preparations, I forgot to say it. That always bothered me. More than two decades later, this book has given me a chance to make that right.

———•———

In April 1998, our Paradigm Records label, which had a broadly commercial scope, released the soundtrack to *The Young and the Restless* TV soap opera as it celebrated its twenty-fifth anniversary.

I attended a *Y&R*-sponsored party at the vaunted Rainbow Room on the sixty-fifth floor of Rockefeller Center, a star-studded stomping ground. I flew to Los Angeles for another anniversary event, this time held on a soundstage at CBS Television City. Beautiful cast members posed for photographers as we hyped the release. A far cry from limping into a truck stop in the Rockies with Discharge.

———•———

On one of our trips to Los Angeles, David and I were sitting in the lobby of the Sunset Marquis. Wolin and I continued our easy camaraderie. Our conversation shifted to famous musicians. David started to detail stories he'd heard about Joe Cocker's notorious behavior and disreputable antics.

I was looking at him anxiously, wide-eyed. I tried to subtly indicate a man seated to our right, his back to us. Wolin didn't take the physical cue, and continued his otherwise entertaining patter. Finally, he took my meaning.

Hooray for Hollywood. The gritty-voiced singer, Cocker, was coincidentally seated right next to us. Wolin froze, and turned so red I thought he was having a stroke.

———•———

In June, we released Shonen Knife's second full-length Big Deal CD, *Happy Hour*. We organized a "livestream"; flying in from Japan, the band would set up in the Microsoft Studios in Redmond, Washington, and give a performance to launch the album. Microsoft had a history with the group. They had previously used Shonen Knife's spirited punk-pop cover of the Carpenters' "Top of the World" in its commercial for Windows 95.

The event was promoted as "the first-ever debut of a new album by a band via the Internet." I still don't know if this was true, but if Microsoft was saying it, we promoted it thus. It also doubled as a kick-off for Windows 98. The video/audio was streamed via Microsoft's "NetShow" technology.

Video on the web was not yet commonly supported. Hardly anyone had the ability to watch moving images on the internet. When you *did* attempt to view something, it was usually a choppy mess. A frustrating minute or two was all most people could muster. Companies were scrambling to develop the dominant video technology in the market.

At the PAL office, I joined our staffers for the late-night broadcast. The computer network, which we shared with PME, was always wonky. With all the talk surrounding our parent company's technological foresight, we still couldn't get the video to broadcast. It was the equivalent of whacking at a black and white television in 1949, trying to clear up the picture. I headed over to the Coyote.

I heard the Shonen Knife show went well. We announced that more than 1,800 people logged in. (Again, I still don't know if this was true.) Our press release about the whole endeavor drew a lot of attention.

———•———

Someone from Tower Records called me and said they wanted to feature Big Deal in *bounce*, its Japanese in-house promotional publication. (*Pulse!* was Tower's US version.) They were impressed with how well Big Deal's import CDs were selling in Japan.

Bounce ran a full-color, Japanese-language piece for which I was interviewed. It highlighted many Big Deal artists and was an obviously complimentary article. I was so busy, I never got it translated.

Still, wanting to take advantage of the coverage, I sent out promotional packages to Japanese labels containing the article, CDs, and press kits detailing our imprints. I followed up and made appointments in Tokyo to discuss licensing opportunities.

Not wanting to be perceived as a *gaijin* ("foreigner" or "outsider"), I immersed myself in local business customs. I read that Japanese businesspeople tend to deliver bad news indirectly, signaling a "no" with body language or with subtler words. I knew not to shake hands unless one was extended, and to give and receive business cards with two hands—and never stuff one into your pocket immediately. I also brought small gifts to exchange.

I flew to Tokyo at the end of July. Sweat soaking through my shirt, I made the rounds. (The one thing I hadn't checked was the weather.) Despite my cultural preparedness, I heard the word "no" said directly ... many times.

Over the weekend I planned to hit the Fuji Rock Festival—Japan's first large-scale outdoor contemporary music event. Shonen

Knife was performing on a bill that included Beck, Elvis Costello, Iggy Pop, and dozens of others. Now in its second year, the multi-day concert was trying to correct some issues it had during its debut.

In August 1997, the fest was inaugurated at the base of Mt. Fuji. Not inconsequentially, it was the height of typhoon season, and on the first day, one struck. After a number of attendees were treated for exposure, and considering the sustained winds and lashing rain, the rest of the event was canceled.

The promoters persevered. For its second year, the Fuji Rock Festival, retaining the original name though held nowhere near its namesake, was taking place at Bayside Square on Tokyo's waterfront August 1st and 2nd.

On Saturday morning, I took a cab to the concert site. The heat and humidity were already stifling. Instead of a mad American-style rush across the wharf to stake out spots for the music, the Japanese ticket holders organized and maintained a long, straight line as they trudged to the staging area. I joined it. I was dressed in black. With the uncomfortable temperatures and yes, more sweat, I was thinking I should have worn something else.

About two minutes into the slog, I was getting very thirsty. I'll grab some water once I get backstage, I thought. Why does my head hurt, I wondered—I didn't drink that much last night. I'm a little unsteady. Dizzy. My heart is racing. My tongue feels weird. I'm nauseous. Oh my god, I quickly realized, I'm probably experiencing heatstroke.

Off in the distance, across a field, I miraculously discerned a soda vending machine outside a utility shack. I wobbled towards it, afraid I would pass out in the unkempt grass. Arriving, I was confronted by an array of unfamiliar Japanese beverages. Did I mention I don't speak Japanese? I fumbled for cash and coins, throwing money into the slots and pounding on every button. A cascade of cans poured out. I chugged everything I could get my hands on and eventually I was able to right myself to some degree. I decided to forgo the entertainment and went back to my hotel.

Later that evening, well-hydrated and recovered, I dined in the hotel's elegant fifty-second floor restaurant. As streaks of lightning darted dramatically across the night sky, I wondered how the festival was going. I learned it was a success, though it turned out others also found the heat unbearable; concertgoers had to be hosed down throughout the day.

Still determined to find its literal sweet spot, the Fuji Rock Festival relocated the following year to a mountain ski resort. (Again, nowhere near Mt. Fuji.) It now flourishes, drawing over 100,000 visitors a year, who I'm guessing do not generally require emergency medical treatment.

At JVC Victor, a record division of the long-established Japanese electronics giant, I met with Katz Ueda and Aya Ohi, young executives who had experience dealing with foreign music markets. Aya had been educated in the States.

I arrived at their air-conditioned office, sweat pouring down my face. I sank into a chair in the waiting room, gulping in the cold air. The two record-people didn't seem to notice, and immediately suggested we go downstairs to an outdoor café. I was sweating so much, I thought I might be having a cardiac event, yet cheerily agreed.

Back outside, they laid out the promotional packet that I'd sent them. I guzzled ice water and began my pitch. They pushed the CDs and press clips around in front of themselves, occasionally speaking in a soft voice to one another in Japanese so as not to interrupt me but still share a pertinent detail.

When Katz came across the *bounce* article, he pointed to a passage, smiled, and said something in his native tongue. Aya smiled and nodded approvingly.

"What interested you there?" I asked.

"Oh," Aya said, "it says you used to work for Noise Records."

Unsure of whether this was a good thing, I cautiously asked if they knew Noise.

"Oh, yes. We distribute Karl's records here in Japan. They sell wonderfully."

"Yes," Katz said, "we should be able to do something with Big Deal."

Having heard the word "no" so many times, I assumed this was finally the indirect "no" I was told to expect.

"OK, well, thanks for having me." We stood up and exchanged parting pleasantries.

"I'll send you our proposal in a few days," Katz said. "We'll pick half a dozen releases to start with."

I said my goodbyes, and headed to the hotel, triumphant. We had a deal to put out our CDs in Japan! Now we were truly international.

Flying home to New York, with an unexpected business-class upgrade, I drank gin and tonics. On my Sony Discman portable CD player, I listened to an advance copy of *Painted from Memory*, a Mercury Records collaboration between Elvis Costello and Burt Bacharach. I looked forward to getting back to the office. That optimism was short-lived.

———•———

Upon my return, David revealed that McPartland told executives at our distributor, ADA, that our label group would be shut down in January.

We confronted McPartland. He said sharing the news with our distributor first was "in the best interests of the shareholders." He confirmed that TCI preferred to focus on the more speculative and ephemeral "products" SonicNet provided.

Turns out Big Deal and Paradigm Associated Labels had to be torn down to make room for the electronic superhighway. It was a huge lesson, and a key to understanding the new, digital-based economy.

In a nutshell: Our solid, growing label was not as attractive as a pie-in-the sky internet venture with hardly any income, but which, in theory, had the possibility to make untold sums. I was apparently hanging on to my quaint notions of how to achieve profitability, or even what "profitability" meant.

The name of the game now was to take a company public, hype the stock, and *then* figure out a way to make money. Survival in this "new economy" meant having a massive "burn-rate"—the ability to spend a lot of cash, post huge losses and show nothing but *potential* for making money. Big Deal became a small component in what was basically a smoke-and-mirrors internet gamble.

In the record business, even the hint that a label is closing often spells disaster. Almost immediately, ADA stopped selling our releases; they even whispered about our impending demise to retailers. As news spread about our closing, CD returns started flooding in. With TCI tightening our purse strings, we were being strangled.

———•———

One morning in September 1998, I drank coffee and watched CNBC's electronic ticker tape slide across the TV screen. TCI Music stock was trading below $4. I reached for the phone.

I dumped most of my stock and picked up just under $100,000. I paid off my debts, and put the remaining $60,000 back into the market.

The mainstream media had embraced everything "internet." *Internet fever* gripped America. It was like the Wild West. Investors were losing their heads in a stampeding bull market. When a company announced anything even remotely internet-related, or an IPO contained ".com" in its name, the stock price would skyrocket. And in this "gold rush" climate, I wasn't immune to stock market speculating.

Online, I could buy 1,000 shares of a touted stock while eating breakfast, walk to work, and sell it forty-five minutes later, after a fifteen-point price jump. Over the next several months, with a series of mainly internet and technology-related trades, I turned my stake into nearly $200,000.

My spirit and passion for music collided with the greed and opportunism of the dot-com-crazed '90s. I used to read the music trades every morning. Now stacks of *The Wall Street Journal* obscured them and copies of *Barron's* littered my floor. I was losing sight of what I had set out to do.

———•———

I was fortunate to work in an industry I enjoyed. It wasn't always about the money. As a fan I've had many experiences and attended hundreds of concerts, many long since forgotten. A few, though, are indelibly stamped in my memory, and, like my love of pop culture in general, they helped form who I am.

In the mid-'70s, the Allman Brothers Band reached peak popularity, almost exclusively playing stadiums and arenas. I was 13. I somehow snagged two fifth-row tickets for the December 8, 1975, show in Buffalo on their *Win, Lose or Draw* tour. I asked one of the prettiest and most popular girls in our middle school to join me; I went to the concert with my dad. People assumed he was a narc. Lead Allman bro Gregg's wife Cher was at the gig. I could see her from my excellent vantage point; she sat on a road case at stage left for the entire performance. A handwritten sign taped to Allman's organ read "Happy Birthday Greg" (sic). It was his 28th. The papers photographed the couple at a disco with our biggest local celebrity, Buffalo Bills running back O.J. Simpson. I still have the program, ticket stub, and press clips.

In early to mid-'79, while I was still in high school, Supertramp's *Breakfast in America* album was everywhere. It spawned four US hit singles, "The Logical Song," "Goodbye Stranger," "Take the Long Way Home," and "Breakfast in America." The album sold four million copies in the US and went to number one around the globe.

They were coming to town. Two girls at school, best friends, both of whom I liked, were really into the UK band and told me they wanted to meet the group. As Dad had recently opened a new gourmet hamburger joint, I obligingly suggested we try to find the stars when they got in, and offer them a free meal and drinks, which we would happily host.

Every music fan knew the one hotel where the top artists stayed. On the day of the band's performance, the three of us headed there. I was armed with an advertisement for my dad's place—it featured a map with its easy-to-find location in a first-ring Buffalo suburb. A palm tree shot up from the restaurant's logo, mirroring the one used by '70s soft-rockers Pablo Cruise. It hinted at the cool California vibe that awaited customers.

Within minutes of arriving at the hotel, the girls had excitedly spotted a few actual band members hanging out in the plant-and-sun-filled atrium. I strode over to their table, the two breathless young ladies trailing right behind. "Hi, sorry to disturb you. We're big fans of yours," I said. Bet they never heard that one before. I handed them the flyer. "My father owns a restaurant. We'd like to invite you for a complimentary meal and drinks before or after your show." I emphasized the drinks and the full bar. My two silent friends were smiling from ear to ear.

They took us kids seriously, and were very nice. "Thanks. We're busy until after the gig, but we appreciate it. Maybe we can stop by then," the spokes-musician said. I thanked him and said we'd hope to see them there.

Dad reluctantly agreed to stay open to accommodate me, somewhat sympathetic to the raging hormones likely driving this preposterous plan.

Regrettably, we didn't have tickets for the sold-out show, but later in the evening, the girls and I staked out some seats at the restaurant. Under the glare of a few staffers who had been pressed into service well past their usual working hours, we waited. Every time the door opened, our hopes for the band's arrival rose, then were cruelly dashed. Nothing. No calls. No band. Dad sent everyone home around 1 a.m.

The next day, the news was filled with stories of Supertramp. Not with reviews, as you might suspect. No, the papers conveyed a tale of the British hitmakers commandeering the minibus they had been provided and tossing their local driver onto the street—a mile or so from our restaurant. They then dropped by a neighborhood tavern, seeking directions back to their hotel, and stayed to have a few beers with workers from the nearby Chevy plant. Having the good sense to realize they could be in a bit of trouble, the group hired an attorney in the early morning hours and turned themselves into police. Giving their side of the story, the authorities said the band claimed: "The driver kept stopping at bars even though they told her they wanted to go to their hotel." No charges were filed.

I like to think they were attempting to visit us before the transportation situation broke down. And all was not in vain. I ended up dating both ladies, separately. They each married musicians.

Live, I watched Bon Scott front AC/DC on October 17, 1979, with an audience of about 2,500 people. He died four months later, at only 33.

I saw the Who at Buffalo's War Memorial Auditorium. It was the day directly after the devastating December 3, 1979, show in Cincinnati where eleven people were killed in a crowd surge at the door. (Years later Pete Townshend expressed regret for performing the Buffalo concert.)

Harvey & Corky Productions was the leading rock promoter in Buffalo through the mid-1970s and early '80s. Harvey is Harvey Weinstein. Yes, *that* "Harvey." Buffalo was where he also began to present niche films that started him on his path as a Hollywood *macher* and felon.

I frequently attended shows at Harvey & Corky's Stage One, a small suburban club minutes from where I grew up. They would bring in developing, early-stage artists, assuring dibs on the acts when they were more popular and could fill larger venues. In the intimate space, I saw performers like John (Cougar) Mellencamp, Squeeze, Pat Benatar, the Police, and Joe Jackson. A few standout memories from Stage One included a show by the Members. I got myself a great spot in front of the stage; it was unbeknownst to me that both the group and the audience would be "participating" during their song "Stand Up and Spit." I kicked around a soccer ball with Irish band the Undertones in the parking lot after their set.

On their first US tour, another Irish band you might have heard of, U2, played a notable show at Stage One. They *opened* for a popular local group, Talas, in December of 1980. There were about 20 people in the club. If everyone who says they were there actually had been, they would have needed an arena that evening. That night, I was home watching *Monday Night Football*, when Howard Cosell announced that John Lennon had been killed in NYC. U2 returned for another performance shortly thereafter, their debut album in ascendancy, and their second just out. They were headlining larger clubs. I was in the audience, as Bono spat, "Where's your fucking Talas now?" After U2 had become one of the biggest bands on Earth, Bono again brought up Talas at a sold-out stadium concert in the Buffalo area. This time, he offered the recollection as more of a reminiscence rather than his earlier, angry fulmination. By then he could afford to let go of the indignity.

I joyously witnessed the Pretenders' first American tour date supporting their debut album release. It was March 12, 1980 at Buffalo State College's Union Social Hall. The group rented the hall for several days prior, testing equipment and rehearsing. Chronologies often cite later gigs as the band's first US show. I saw them twice that year, in their original lineup, with late members James Honeyman-Scott and Peter Farndon.

I've been lucky to see Paul Weller in three incarnations: with the Jam, the Style Council, and as a solo artist.

I was in the audience at London's ICA December 29, 1984; the recently formed Scottish band the Jesus and Mary Chain played a 15-minute set that devolved into ear-splitting feedback as they left the stage. Half the crowd was in awe. The other half sought refunds. The sold-out appearance is a seminal event in their history. And it was precisely this type of thing that, three months later, would lead to a full-scale riot at one of their shows—and a series of gold records.

Graham Parker gave one of the most exciting live performances I've ever seen, August 3, 1985, at Pier 84 in New York City. I still crack up when I think of Paul Rudd's music industry character in *This is 40*. A passionate Parker fan, he was banking his entire record label on a comeback album for the justifiably mythologized singer-songwriter.

And, after serving a three-year prison sentence for cocaine possession and assault, Rick James delivered an astonishing, clear-eyed show at midsize club Tramps in New York City on January 3, 1998. It was his first tour in ten years, and his first concert in Manhattan since playing the world-famous Harlem theater, the Apollo in 1991. Every person in the room, including myself, was dancing from the opening number to the last. (Back in the day, James, a Buffalo native, used to stop by the Continental occasionally. I would have a chin-wag and smoke a joint with him and his entourage on the club's back patio.)

———•———

Angling to keep the business alive, Wolin and I discussed buying Paradigm Associated Labels from TCI. Under Charlie Pye's guidance, we put an offer together, and presented it to McPartland.

The basic deal was that we would take over the company for the assumption of its debts, which were close to $250,000. McPartland laughed in our faces and said there was no way he would present that to TCI. We countered with a $200,000 cash offer on top of the debt assumption.

McPartland said he couldn't sell it to us because we were not "qualified buyers"—we didn't have deep enough pockets. Maybe that was true, but it still hurt to be told we were not qualified to buy the company we'd founded and run for the last several years.

McPartland again said he was acting in the best interest of the shareholders. Frustrated, we went out and sought a "qualified" investor to partner with.

Meanwhile, I raced to make sure our new friends at JVC Victor got everything they needed to manufacture the Big Deal releases in

Japan. If we *were* able to continue the label, I wanted to ensure that the relationship was in good shape. And, if the label *didn't* make it, I wanted the artists to at least have the opportunity and thrill of seeing their CDs released in Japan.

I rushed to get the Merrymakers' *Bubblegun* CD out in the States before everything started to fall apart. We had licensed the melodic Swedish group's album from Virgin Records. The key band members came to NYC to meet us and do some promotion in advance of the release. I kept up appearances as I wined and dined them; the evening ended with many shots at the Coyote. At the office the next day, I hoped their hangovers would prevent them from picking up on what was happening behind the scenes.

Big Deal had recently released *The Apple Bed* by Nick Heyward (of Haircut 100), licensed from Creation Records in the UK. Heading into the Thanksgiving weekend, Creation founder Alan McGee, another industry hero of mine, called to thank me for the work we were doing for Heyward. He was in New York and asked to get together. Much to my regret, I had plans and was on my way out the door.

I was grateful for his call. It highlighted all we had achieved— and the possibilities that might never lie ahead. I was hopeful and engaged in finding a way out of our predicament, and desperately wanted to continue to grow the label group, but the logical part of me said we had reached the end of the line.

As Christmas approached, McPartland told us he planned to fire our entire staff. TCI higher-ups in Colorado got wind of it and insisted that he follow certain corporate procedures, including waiting until after the New Year to can everyone in one swoop. For once, bureaucracy worked in our favor.

Conducting meetings through the holidays, we continued the search for an investor. Wolin scored a candidate from California: Henry Marx, owner of a jazz label called Sin-Drome Records. Marx agreed to buy Paradigm Associated Labels even before meeting us, which I felt was odd. But he and Wolin hit it off over the phone.

No big deal: 1999

Marx drafted a letter of intent in early January 1999. As the TCI hatchet people were about to board their plane for New York City to conduct exit interviews and do away with our employees, Wolin hovered over the fax machine, waiting for Marx's signed offer. When it chugged out, he ripped it off and flew upstairs. With the backing of Marx's business holdings to qualify it, his offer of $200,000 plus the assumption of the debt was accepted.

TCI had shut off all monies except salaries. Creditors had gone unpaid, and relationships were strained. It was impossible to explain to our artists the nuances of what was happening. I kept a brave public face, but I'd become uncertain we could recover. In the nearly four months since David and I presented our original offer, the labels' debt ballooned to nearly $450,000.

Yet, I agreed to get together with Marx and Wolin when our new "partner" flew in the following week. Meeting the gruff, heavy-set Brooklyn transplant in person didn't ease the unsettled feelings I already had about him and the deal. The bad vibe continued through lunch.

He and Wolin did all the talking. Marx asked me why I was so quiet. I told him of a Sicilian expression I'd heard that roughly translated as, "To speak little is a beautiful art." The check arrived. Marx barked for me to pick it up. Now, another expression came to mind—this time Yiddish slang: "chazzer." With a forced smile,

I said, "Fine … you buy the company … I'll buy lunch." He didn't laugh.

It was a bad start, and I couldn't shake the sense that something was wrong.

We proceeded with meetings: that afternoon, as we introduced Marx to McPartland, the executive lavished praise on me and Wolin. He explained that PAL was on the block because TCI Music, now a different company, simply didn't want to be in the record business.

Marx, Wolin, and I arranged to meet for coffee at the Soho Grand Hotel with our lawyers the next morning to go over paperwork and discuss plans. At the table, I still couldn't shake my dislike of Marx. I had spent my entire professional life avoiding guys like this—showbiz caricatures. Hold on. Did he just say he wants to sign Jethro Tull? What is going on here? My stomach churned through the whole meeting.

I finally decided to participate in the conversation, and made a comment.

Marx turned to me and said, "Why don't you shut up and let the attorneys deal with it." This was the first time I had actually put two sentences together since meeting the guy.

The lawyers left and we hit the sidewalk. Wolin and Marx chattered about details, then Marx grabbed a cab. Alone with Wolin, I turned to my business partner and said, "I'm out."

He started to say goodbye, thinking I was just leaving.

I said, "No. I mean I'm done. I'm not participating in this buyout. I'm taking my winnings and calling it a day." By not joining them, TCI would have to pay out my contract. So, I'd also get a year's salary. To emphasize the moment, I brushed my hands together like Vegas casino dealers when they leave the table, and that was that.

———•———

TCI and Marx eventually closed their deal. TCI had by then agreed to sell PAL to Marx, the "qualified buyer," solely for the assumption of the debt.

TCI Music's stock price had remained virtually unchanged in the five months since I had sold my shares. Wolin sold his stock around this time. He needed the cash to buy a townhouse in Brooklyn.

In March of 1999, in a complex deal, AT&T purchased Tele-Communications Inc. for $55 billion. TCI Music, one of the many assets, divisions, and investments of Tele-Communications Inc. was absorbed by AT&T. It had little impact on TCI Music stock—for the moment.

Remember the ".com" boost I mentioned earlier? About a month later, TCI executives engineered one of the greatest one-day stock price gains of all time, based solely on a press release. They announced that their various companies' "digital" assets—including the TCI Music portfolio—were merging; the new company name was Liberty Digital.

With the internet stock market frenzy in full swing, Liberty Digital (TCI Music) stock moved up nearly *900 percent* on the announcement. Veteran financial writer Christopher Byron (*Bloomberg News, Forbes, The New York Observer*) called it a "conjurer's trick" and said the company's action was no more significant than "taking money out of one's left pocket and putting it into the right one." If Wolin and I had held on to our shares, we could have sold them the next day for $2 million each.

Now, if you think I shrugged off this whole episode, you'd be mistaken. The evening after the stock jumped, I was headed to Gallaghers to meet a group of friends for a previously arranged dinner. In the cab on the way to the restaurant, I replayed my decision to sell early over and over. How did I not see this coming? All management had to do was utter the magic word "internet" and start bagging the loot. I *had* been speculating on every dot-com wannabe out there. What if, rather than getting caught up in the market madness, I'd been more patient? *If I had only not listened to so-and-so ... If only I'd done nothing.* During the meal, I was a zombie. The music business friends I was dining with couldn't comprehend my situation. They were likely having a good old time, talking shop, making jokes. Carrying on as usual. I didn't hear a thing. I took a hit and it hurt. It was a gut punch. One that would take months to recover from. Sure, I had done well, and had a few bucks; I wasn't worried about much. But, well you get it. I left $2 million on the table.

McPartland, who'd earned millions for himself and many around him, resigned from Liberty Digital weeks later.

Charlie Pye, our accountant, had quietly held on to *his* shares. He sold after this market event, and moved his family to Kentucky, where he became a minister. I might have dedicated myself to God, too, if I'd pocketed the $2 million.

———•———

After paying the taxman, I had enough to live on for a couple of years. I embarked on an extended self-guided tour that included the bars and racetracks of Miami and New Orleans. I then returned to my "office" at the Coyote Ugly Saloon.

———•———

In mid-1999, Liberty Digital sold SonicNet and Addicted to Noise to MTV Networks in a deal that was publicized as "creating the world's largest online music company." The acquisition was meant to "harness MTV's disparate online assets and transform MTV into a major player in online music." SonicNet CEO Nicholas Butterworth became the head of a newly created MTV Interactive (MTVi) Group. Liberty Digital retained a stake in this new undertaking. The fact is that MTVi was formed partly so Viacom, MTV's parent, would have the possibility of creating an internet IPO spinoff to cash in on the sector's astronomical stock market rise over the past two years. It was the same as the "Liberty Digital" scam: still with no profits to show, these guys were trying to pull it off again!

———————◆———————

Wolin stuck it out with Marx. By October, the two officially and permanently shut down Paradigm Associated Labels. They couldn't make it work. Wolin filed suit against AT&T, TCI, Liberty Digital, et al. for defamation of character and his employee stock options. (We never saw those options McPartland had promised us.) TCI countered, denying all claims. Wolin settled out of court. Marx sued as well, claiming TCI misrepresented the value of PAL before he purchased it. TCI counter-sued Marx, but somehow ended up *paying him* to settle and take the whole label group away.

I lost interest in the minutiae. But, while writing this, I looked up Marx on the web. Over two decades later, he has a website for a company called "Big Deal Records." We never used the word "records." The site shows our old logo, with the extra word shabbily added underneath. The first words on the "About Us" page are:

"Big Deal
Records was founded by Henry Marx ..."

Tick, tick, tick, boom: 2000-2001

Audio streaming service provider Napster launched in mid-1999, and by then, all hell had broken loose in the music business. Global sales were down for the first year that anyone could remember. Napster's technology allowed users to access music from other users' computers, downloading MP3 music files directly from each other's hard drives. In March of 2000 the Napster community had twenty million people drawing from over four million available songs. By summer, Napster users were downloading 14,000 free songs every minute.

The digital music revolution had begun in earnest, sparking a full-scale restructuring of the record industry. We'd all known it was coming, though collectively and predictably, the business was in denial, and slow to react. The advent of peer-to-peer file-sharing anticipated the future, where *musicians* released recordings themselves, rather than waiting for archaic things like *record companies* to bring their music to market.

Most visibly, Metallica brought a lawsuit against Napster in California. It focused on copyright infringement, racketeering, and unlawful use of digital audio interface devices. Metallica drummer Lars Ulrich testified before the Senate Judiciary Committee, decrying the blatant theft of their music. The Recording Industry Association of America (RIAA) sued Napster and nearly 20,000 actual software users.

———•———

The dot-com bubble burst in 2000. Companies like Pets.com, Kozmo, Webvan, and hundreds of others both public and private disappeared, burning through their capital before attaining profitability. The fever had broken; the focus on rampant speculation and growth over profits seemed to be settling down.

Instead of achieving its envisioned gilded stock offering, MTVi had become a money pit yielding few tangible benefits. The IPO was scrubbed. "There's not a reason on earth that we would spin off something if the market isn't going to appreciate the value of it,' Viacom's new president, Mel Karmazin said in a late-2000 investor earnings call.

A little over a year after the SonicNet purchase, 25 percent of the MTVi staff was laid off and new executives were installed above Butterworth. The MTVi unit limped along until 2002. Through all the mergers and acquisitions involving MTV, Viacom, Warner, CBS, and Paramount companies over the decades, a legacy of its multi-million-dollar investment in the entity encompassing SonicNet and Addicted to Noise remains. Enter "sonicnet.com" in your browser and you'll find yourself forwarded to VH1's website. Addictedtonoise.com sends you to MTV.com.

———————•———————

In the early days of the Coyote, one of my favorite bartenders had been Elizabeth Gilbert. The funny and highly intelligent Gilbert had ambition that extended well beyond the bar. She was a writer, and had penned a story for *GQ* in 1997 called "The Muse of the Coyote Ugly Saloon." (Subhead: *She'll pour for you; you'll pour your heart out to her. Confessions of a girl bartender at Lil's joint*). It detailed her time at my local. Yes, the article mentions "Big Daddy."

When Liz's writing career took off, she stopped working at the Coyote. She still popped into the bar from time to time, with her then-husband or a few pals. We always talked. Among the friends in her orbit was Jana Eisenberg, a sparky newspaper writer with a great smile. I bumped into her at the Coyote occasionally and ran into her at Elaine's, the noted literary hangout, when Liz had an event there.

Gilbert sold her *GQ* Coyote story to producer Jerry Bruckheimer. Like many adaptations, *Coyote Ugly*, the movie, had little to do with the actual article—or the bar for that matter.

I'm still not sure why—maybe because I knew Liz, or had spent enough time at the bar—I was invited to the film's premier at the Ziegfeld Theatre on 54th Street, right next to my old TRA office. It was the summer of 2000.

Post-screening, there was a lavish after-party at Roseland Ballroom. Celebrities at the bash included Hugh Jackman, Tyra Banks, Christopher Meloni, Mariska Hargitay, Maria Bello, Bridget Moynahan, Justin Timberlake and members of NSYNC, and LeAnn Rimes.

Jana and Liz were hanging out. Gilbert had a *New York Times* reporter trailing her. Liz greeted me with an effusive, "Big Daddy!" Yep, you guessed it. That weekend my name was in a *Times* article about Liz's evening—well, not exactly. I was referred to as "Big Daddy."

I found Jana by the bar later (that's a sentence that's still heard about her) and this time, planted a kiss on her. We've been together over twenty years.

Seems like significant events happened for me at Roseland.

———•———

In this transitory period in the music and online worlds, I tried to get a few projects off the ground. A new record label. An online media company. The landscape was shifting underfoot, and everyone was trying to figure out how it was all going to work. I struggled to find a professional path to get excited about.

On September 11, 2001, a big plane flew directly over my head and crashed into a really big building.

A few months later, Jana and I are sitting at the Coyote Ugly. The bar, despite our efforts to deny it, had changed into a parody of itself. The tourists had arrived.

I realized that it's almost five years to the date since McPartland told me that we "could at least look forward to a great quality of life for the next five years." We considered our options.

It was definitely time to go. Not just leave the bar—but leave this town.

Round trip to Buffalo: 2002-present

Jana and I got married in the spring of 2002, a month before we both turned 40. Liz gave the toast at our wedding party.

(In 2006, Elizabeth Gilbert released her fourth book, her first memoir, called *Eat, Pray, Love*. The global success of the book stunned her and everyone. It sold twelve million copies. It was translated into thirty languages and made into another bad movie—though, Liz quipped, she'd gotten quite the upgrade with Julia Roberts portraying "Liz" in the film.)

One year after 9/11, we returned to my hometown, Buffalo, NY, to live.

Hearkening back to my earlier collecting, buying, and selling habits, I became an art dealer. I specialized in art and artworks with a direct connection to Buffalo and Western New York—still working with creatives, but in decidedly more genteel surroundings.

In the early part of the twentieth century, as Buffalo's grain, steel and other industries and businesses prospered, the community was very supportive of the arts; as a result, there's a rich history of art produced during the previous century.

The shrewd collecting instincts of patrons like A. Conger Goodyear (1877-1964) and Seymour H. Knox, Jr. (1898-1990)—and their donations—led to the Albright Art Gallery (later the Albright-Knox Art Gallery, and now the Buffalo AKG Art Museum) possessing one of the country's most impressive and presciently developed modern and abstract art collections.

Much later, in the 1970s, parallel with the period of American Rust Belt decline, and Buffalo no exception, a nexus of creative visual art, literature, and musical activity arose. Much of it was due to arts funding from Governor Nelson Rockefeller's administration, as well as financial support from the New York State Council on the Arts and the National Endowment for the Arts. It wasn't enough to keep many of these *artistes*, or others around, though many notable art greats were formed, taught, or began their careers here. Robert Longo and Cindy Sherman went to college and worked in the city. Pioneers like Tony Conrad, Hollis Frampton, Paul Sharits, Steina and Woody Vasulka, all associated with the University at Buffalo, led the way for experimental film and digital video. Wunderkind Michael Tilson Thomas (following musical visionary Lukas Foss) took the helm of the Buffalo Philharmonic Orchestra. In these environments, painters and photographers flourished, producing bodies of work that remained in the region. By the time of my return, their paintings and prints had started to find a solid collector's base.

It was bizarre being back, but it suited our middle-aged and underemployed aspirations of ease and affordability. Jana got to work as a freelance writer.

In 2008, we were featured in a *New York* magazine article about the reemergence of Buffalo. We were photographed in our elegant condo—much nicer than we would have been able to afford in NYC, and quoted as saying we missed the restaurants, but not the lifestyle.

As Jana explored, made friends, and tried to figure out how she wound up in Buffalo, I wondered the same thing. The town had changed, but not much. The Continental was razed in 2009; there was a pile of rubble where it had stood, and someone opened a boutique hotel on the site.

Buffalo was trying mightily for a "renaissance." After a decade, I found a local bar to call home. They specialize in craft cocktails. I just drink tequila. They know my name, but don't call me "Big Daddy."

In 2015, my company, Dean Brownrout Modern/Contemporary, presented an exhibition in Buffalo featuring the photographs of the late filmmaker Hollis Frampton, who had spent his last years teaching and working here. It was the first comprehensive showing of Frampton's still photographs in thirty years.

The show was a critical and financial success, receiving press and attention from all over the world. Big city gallerists flew in. We had offers and agreed to an exhibition of Frampton's photos with a hip New York City gallery; the Whitney Museum of American Art quietly purchased the entire New York City show for its collection. I was "back in the bigs."

Subsequent exhibitions in New York City took place. In early 2020, we were scheduling presentations of Frampton's photographs in London and Zurich, when a little virus flew around the world.

If you want to hear what music I'm listening to now, look for me on Spotify.

Epilogue

"You don't know what's going to happen. Big things look like little things. Little things don't have big signs on them that say 'This is a Big Thing.' They look like everything else." This quote from director Mike Nichols pretty much sums up many of my stories.

And I've asked myself, if I'd stuck it out with Steve Martin, would I have become a top agent? I never wanted to be a music agent. I always wanted to be a record guy. If I hadn't sold my stock early, would my life have turned out better? It would be different, certainly. Maybe I'd have ended up a cautionary tale, one of those guys who, with their sudden tech millions, went sailing off a cliff in his new Porsche. How was I to know? I was just making my way in life and the music business, looking for opportunity, following my instincts and learning as I went along.

I made a living and survived—mostly on my own terms—in New York City for nearly twenty years. Some were more enjoyable or profitable than others. I had many great experiences. I traveled. I ate at nice restaurants. I met my wife. In the good record-biz years, giving a break to musicians, releasing albums, and getting them in stores was generally a great feeling. It was a privilege to create opportunities for others to pursue their dreams.

When I returned to Buffalo, a city I couldn't wait to leave in my twenties, I did briefly feel like Henry Hill at the end of *Goodfellas*: "a schnook." I'd left "the life" in NYC, the highs (and the lows).

This made me empathize further with the film's portrayal of Hill, though at least I could get a good plate of spaghetti with marinara sauce. In Buffalo, a famous red-sauce town, it sometimes seemed like that's *all* I could get. Trends like farm-to-table restaurants were decades late in hitting.

There are easier ways to make a living than being an art dealer in Buffalo, NY. There are also worse things I could be doing. But count me as surprised as you that moving back to my hometown would lead to my own version of an American "second act."

Acknowledgments

Jana Eisenberg, whose humor, patience, intelligence, vocabulary, and surgically deft editing hand has been a part of every page.

Will Faller, whose loyalty could serve as a textbook lesson to those who don't possess such a quality.

Megan Lee at M + R, for her gift of listening that, in no small measure, inspired me to write this.

Michael Mirolla and Guernica Editions for the opportunity.

Those whose comments, contributions, and/or recollections helped shape this book: David Gehlke, David Halpern, Steve Martin, Gerald Mead, Joshua Melville, Ira Robbins, Chris Schobert, Michael Shelley, Kevin Somers, and David Wolin.

Alan Lord, for your newfound support and generosity. Thanks for pushing me past the finish line.

A special acknowledgment to Howard Enis aka Cal Zone. In the early years, as a DJ and music director for Buffalo State College radio station WBNY, and then as an employee at Celluloid in NYC, Cal championed the local bands and individuals he befriended as a college student. Without his support, the lives of so many people, including myself, would have taken a decidedly different path. Cal's enthusiasm for music abides. He is currently a DJ on WAYO 104.3 in Rochester, NY. And his eldest son, Eli, carries on the music-related family tradition as a writer, contributing to publications including *Rolling Stone*, *Billboard*, and *Entertainment Weekly*.

Warm thanks to those who *were* or *are* part of the journey—in positive measures small and large. You are appreciated: Tommy Allen, Alan Atkinson, Eric Bartels, Sherry Bogen, Marty Boratin, Nancy Brennan, Arne Brogger, Whitney Broussard, Bud Burke,

Janz Castelo, Yana Chupenko, Ron Colinear, Mike Connelly, Mark Corsi, John DeNicola, Tom Derr, Rachel Dodd, Alan Donatelli, Katherine Dovlatov, Dawn Eden, Leona Faber, Loren Falls, Mark Falls, Jimmy Ford, Dave Frey, Casey Fundaro, Gerry Gerrard, Elizabeth Gilbert, Geordie Gillespie, Scott Givens, Harold Goldberg, Scott Grodnick, Don Grossinger, Brad Jones, Ivan Julian, Anne Katzenbach, Geoff Kelly, Doug Keogh, Bruce Kirkland, Steve Knutson, Karl Kotas, James Kyllo, Holly Lane, John Lay, Elizabeth Licata, Morgan Lieberthal aka Mr. Morgan, Liliana Lovell, Francis Macdonald, Tim Marback, Phil McWalter, Fred Mett, Jerri Meyer, Albie Michaels, David Patrick Mitchell, Chris Monlux, Jan Mullen, Kathy Nizzari, Laura Norden, Jordan Oakes, George Paaswell, Steven Parelman, Catherine Parker, David Perelstein, Peter Primont, Charles Pye, Mike Quinn, Evie Rabeck, Rights of the Accused, Dalton Ross, Steve Salem, Richard Sanders, Felix Sebacious, Laura Silverman, Bob Singerman, Gary Sperrazza, Jacqui Squatriglia, Karl Walterbach, and Steven Wren.

Special thanks to worldradiohistory.com and Espolòn Tequila Blanco as invaluable resources.

Bibliography

Anderson, Dale. "Allman Bros. Band Makes It a Happy Return on Gregg's Birthday," *Buffalo Evening News*, December 9, 1975

Armao, Lauren. "A History of Sub Pop Records," *Fluorescent Magazine*, July 6, 2021

Associated Press. "CDs Overtake LPs for First Time, Industry Says," January 26, 1989

Barnard, Christopher. "One Last Party at the Jane Hotel," *New York Times*, November 23, 2022

Beatty, Sally. "MTV Lays Off 25% of Online Unit, Cancels Plans for Public Offering," *The Wall Street Journal*, September 28, 2000

Bennet, James. "Motive is Puzzle in Fatal Pool-Hall Rampage," *New York Times*, March 1, 1992

BettingUSA.com. "Superfecta Bet"

Buhrmester, Jason. "Against the Grain: The Oral History of Epitaph Records," *Spin.com*, October 19, 2010

Byron, Christopher. "TCI Music Benefits From a Little Internet Alchemy," *TheStreet.com*, April 14, 1999

Gage, Nicholas. "A Nightclub Owner Says He Has Woes—the Mafia," *New York Times*, October 10, 1974

Goux, Clovis. "RIP Jean Karakos," *Redbullmusicacademy.com*, January 25, 2017

Gray, Christopher. "Popeye Slept Here and Now Olive Oyl Can, Too," *New York Times*, July 14, 2009

Harris, Mark. *Mike Nichols: A Life*, Penguin Press, 2021

Holden, Stephen. "Promoting Lambada," *New York Times*, January 10, 1990

Hu, Jim. "Viacom May Be Reorganizing MTVi Group," *CNET*, January 2, 2002

Lamont, Tom. "Napster: The Day the Music Was Set Free," *The Guardian*, February 23, 2013

Los Angeles Times. "Prison Term for Ex-O.C. Promoter," October 7, 1992

Martino, Alison. "The Tropicana Motel's Totally Rocking Heyday," *Los Angeles magazine*, October 12, 2015

New York Times. "Sid Vicious Arrested for Assault in Disco," December 8, 1978

PageSix.com. "We Hardly Knew Marylou's," August 10, 2007

Philips, Chuck. "Capitol Records Scores Victory in the Bullfight for Matador," *Los Angeles Times*, May 31, 1996

Ray, Lexis-Olivier. "How a Legendary Boxing Arena Became a Lens for Los Angeles," *Hyperallergic*, February 24, 2021

Relix. "40 Years Ago Today, The Grateful Dead Drew Over 125,000 to Raceway Park," September 4, 2017

Staas, James. "Rockers Say: Leave Driving to Us," *Buffalo Evening News*, June 8, 1979

TheMarqueeClub.net. "The Wardour St. Days (1964-1988)"

Untapped New York. "20 Buildings in NYC Designed by Architect Stanford White," October 16, 2018

Verna, Paul. "Goo Goo Dolls Sue Label Over Royalties," *Billboard*, December 14, 1996

Wagner, Laura. "'8 CDs for a Penny' Company Files for Bankruptcy," *NPR*, August 11, 2015

Wall Street Journal. "Viacom Unit to Buy SonicNet, The Box in Exchange for Stake," May 20, 1999

Waller, Don. "Metallica Sues Napster for Copyright Violation," *Variety*, April 14, 2000

About the Author

Dean Brownrout was born in the early '60s and raised in the Buffalo, NY area. By the time he was a teenager, with the entrepreneurial bent instilled in him by family, he was promoting rock concerts and managing local bands. It was the era of the burgeoning new wave music movement.

At 21, he moved to New York City to pursue a career in the music business. As a talent agent, he booked a pre-major-label Metallica into New York's Roseland Ballroom for a seminal 1984 show; it led to their signing to Elektra Records.

His experience with the punk, hardcore, and metal genres motivated him to found Mercenary Records in the late 1980s. He signed the now multi-platinum Goo Goo Dolls to their first recording agreement, and released their debut album. In 1993, after a stint running the US operation of German-based heavy metal label, Noise Records, Brownrout cofounded Big Deal, an independent record company, running it out of his Greenwich Village living room. The label, which specialized in power pop, was much more to his personal musical taste. In 1996, he sold Big Deal to an early internet startup. Brownrout continued to run Big Deal as it expanded; it eventually had a dozen employees and released hundreds of recordings worldwide. The combined business was purchased by cable giant Tele-Communications Inc. and then AT&T; he left the company in 1999.

In 2002, Brownrout moved back to Buffalo. He became an art dealer specializing in historically important art of the area. He represents the photographic estate of avant-garde film pioneer Hollis Frampton, and works with galleries and museums around the world. He lives with his wife in Buffalo's Elmwood Village.

Printed by Imprimerie Gauvin
Gatineau, Québec